A SHORT TREATISE

OF THE

ISLE OF MAN

DIGESTED INTO SIX CHAPTERS

By

James Chaloner

ONE OF THE COMMISSIONERS UNDER LORD FAIRFAX,

FOR SETTLING THE AFFAIRS IN THE ISLE OF MAN, IN 1662; AND

AFTERWARDS GOVERNOR OF THE ISLAND, FROM 1658 TO 1660.

ORIGINALLY PUBLISHED IN 1656,

AS AN APPENDIX TO "KING'S VALE ROYAL OF ENGLAND;

OR, THE COUNTY PALATINE OF CHESTER, ILLUSTRATED."

EDITED, WITH AN INTRODUCTORY NOTICE, AND

COPIOUS NOTES, BY THE

REV. J. G. CUMMING, M.A., F.G.S.,

RECTOR OF MELLIS, SUFFOLK; LATE WARDEN, AND PROFESSOR OF

CLASSICAL LITERATURE AND OF GEOLOGY, QUEEN'S COLLEGE, BIRMINGHAM;

FORMERLY VICE-PRINCIPAL OF KING WILLIAM'S COLLEGE, ISLE OF MAN.

A Short Treatise of the Isle of Man by James Chaloner

This edition © 2013 Camrose Media Ltd.

ISBN: 978-1-907945-55-7

Published 2013 by: Lily Publications Ltd, PO Box 33, Ramsey, Isle of Man IM99 4LP.

INTRODUCTORY NOTICE BY THE EDITOR

————————

THE following *Short Treatise of the Isle of Man*, digested into six chapters, written by James Chaloner, was originally printed in folio, by John Streater, in Little Bartholomew's, London, as an Appendix (with a separate title page) to "*The Vale Royal of England; or, the County Palatine of Chester*, illustrated: performed by William Smith and William Webb, Gentlemen," and published by Daniel King, in 1656. The work is very scarce, and when perfect, fetches a high price.

Regarded as a separate treatise, it is the oldest history of the Isle of Man.

Camden, in his *Britannia*, in 1586, had previously given an outline of Manx history, compiled from the *Chronicon Maniae et Insularum* (published in the fourth volume of the Manx Society), and from papers by John Merrick, who was Bishop of Man from 1577 to 1600.

In the *Polychronicon* of Ralph Higden, 1482, there is a brief notice of the Island, in Lib. 1, cap. xv. Thomas Durham, in 1595, published the oldest known separate map of the Island, which was copied by John Speed, in 1610, and re-copied by Daniel King, on a reduced scale, for this work of Chaloner, with the omission of the ships, and the figures of marine animals bearing the standards of the British Isles, and the addition, on the margin of the map, of eight small views in the Isle of Man, and the arms of the Island (the "Tree Cassyn," or three legs), and the arms of Lord Fairfax. The map accompanying the present edition of Chaloner's treatise, is transferred on a still further reduced scale, from this latter copy, and printed by the photozincographic process (as are

GEO. A. DEAN, PHOTO-LITHO, DOUGLAS, ISLE OF MAN.

also the two plates of views, the facsimile of title page, and the plate of arms of the Beaumont family) by Mr. G. A. Dean, of Douglas, Isle of Man.

The portrait of Lord Fairfax, in this volume, transferred by the same process, is taken from a painting by Walker, and is an addition to the book as originally published. The autograph "Fairfax," is from a document bearing his signature, amongst the Records in Rushen Castle in the Isle of Man.

In this edition, the orthography of Chaloner has been preserved; as for instance the perpetual use of *then* for "than," and the forms *Tinewald*, *Tynwald*, and *Tinwald*, on the same page. Where the errors are evidently due to the printer, or to the ignorance of the author in the spelling of Manx names, some corrections have been made. There are indications that Chaloner himself did not see his work through the press. Had he done so, he would hardly have left the addenda and errata in so incomplete a state, or the text with gaps in it where there should be names; these the printer or editor could not perhaps satisfactorily make out from Chaloner's MS.

Had not this volume formed one of the series published by the Manx Society, I should have added largely to the extent of the Notes, by the introduction of many more documents bearing upon Manx history, to which references only are made. These documents, having already been printed in the fourth, seventh, and ninth volumes of the Society, under the laborious and careful editorship of Dr. Oliver, and in the first volume (Sacheverell's *Survey of the Isle ofMan*), edited by myself, seemed to me likely to create a needless expenditure of print if repeated in this.

There will be found in the Appendix several very interesting documents, extracted from the Episcopal and other Registers of the Isle of Man, which have not hitherto appeared in print, and which could not conveniently be introduced into the *Notes*. *Appendix G* is an extension and correction of the extract referred to in *Note* 38.

I have also on the ground of avoiding repetition of the same matter in the series of the *Manx Society*, omitted to make notes in this volume upon several points in the history, manners, and customs of the Isle of Man, which I had previously treated of in vol. i. These volumes (Sacheverell's and Chaloner's Histories), may well be regarded as supplementary to each other, and should be read together. In the latter, I have been able to amend some of the conclusions arrived at in the former from the very imperfect data possessed by me at the time when it was published, the intervening volumes of the Manx Society having afforded more complete materials for the elucidation of the darker periods of Manx history.

This is a proof, amongst many others, of the value to the historian, antiquary, and genealogist, of the Society's publications.

I would take advantage of this introductory notice, to make an amendment on page 107 of this volume, which was printed off before my final corrections were made. I have there spoken of Alan, Lord of Galloway, as being *descended* from Somerled, Thane of Argyle. I should have said *connected with*; and should have added that Affreca, daughter of Fergus, Lord of Galloway, married Olave Kleining, King of Man (son of Godred Crovan), and that an illegitimate daughter of Olave Kleining (Ayla), was married to Somerled, and it was their son, Dugald, who for a time (in 1155), gained the kingdom of the Isles.—(See Appendix B.) Train observes, in his *History of the Isle of Man*, vol. i., p. 123, that when we add to the above circumstances, "That Thomas the Black, son of Alan, married a *daughter* (he should have said *sister*—see Appendix A.) of Godred Don, we may infer that it was probably from these and other connections that the Galloway family became so much interested in the affairs of the Western Islands, and of Man." These same connections afford additional reasons to those mentioned in *Notes* 56, 58, 59, and 61, for the interest taken by the Comyn family in Manx affairs, since both John, the Black Comyn, Lord of Badenoch, and John Comyn, Earl of Buchan, were descended from Alan, Lord of Galloway.—(See *Appendix A.*)

I have stated (*Note* 68), that "the documents pertaining to William Christian (Illiam Dhone), will be given amongst the publications of the Manx Society, under the editorship of my valued friend and quondam pupil, James Brnman, Esq., F.R.A.S., Secretary to H.E., the Lieutenant-Governor of the Isle of Man, and one of the Council of the Society." Whilst the sheet containing that statement was being printed off, this distinguished and deeply-lamented Manxman, was suddenly removed from the scene of his labours. But the arrangement of the documents which he had collected, is in such a state of forwardness, that it is hoped there will be no difficulty in their publication at an early period, under the able editorship of another well-known Member of the Manx Bar.

I must express the deep obligations I am under to Paul Bridson, Esq., one of the Honorary Secretaries of the Manx Society, for several of the documents extracted from the Episcopal, and other Registers of the Isle of Man; and for many notes upon the names of the Clergy of the Island and Officers of Government, in the days of Chaloner. To these notes I have appended the initials P. B.

To Dr. Taylor, of Elgin, the learned author of *Edward the First of England in the North of Scotland*, my hearty thanks are due, for the kindness he has shewn me, in furnishing much information, and many copies of interesting documents illustrative of the connection of Henry de Beaumont and the Comyns, with the Isle of Man.

To Lady Gordon Cumming, of Altyre, and another lady, who wishes to remain anonymous, I am deeply indebted for a great part of the materials of the Genealogical Tables, in the Appendix.

J. G. CUMMING.
Mellis Rectory, Suffolk,
May 1st, 1864.

A Short

TREATISE

O F

The Iſle of MAN.

Digeſted into Six Chapters.

CONTAINING,

I. *A Deſcription of the Iſland.*
II. *Of the Inhabitants.*
III. *Of the State Eccleſiaſticall.*
IIII. *Of the Civill Government.*
V. *Of the Trade.*
VI. *Of the Strength of the Iſland.*

Illuſtrated with Severall *Proſpects*
of the Iſland,

By *Daniel King.*

LONDON,
Printed by *John Streater,* 1656.

FOR HIS EXCELLENCIE, THOMAS LORD FAIRFAX,[1]
LORD OF MAN AND OF THE ISLES.

———————

My Lord,

THE last Year, when Robert Dynely, Esquire, Mr. Joshua Witton, Minister of the Gospel; and my self, your Lordships Commissioners for the settling of your Affairs in the Isle of Man, returned from that Employment; We gave your Lordship an Accompt in Writing, as well as by word of mouth, of our Proceedings there, as in relation to your Revenue, and the Government of the Countrey; so also what our Actings were in pursuance of your pious intentions for the promoting of Religion and Learning; which performed, might in a matter of this nature, be held for a compentent discharge of our Duty; and such constructions your Lordship was pleased to make of it: Neverthelesse, having made (be it said without vanity, or detracting in the least from my Companions) a more then ordinary inquisition into the state of the Island; I held my self obliged to present to your Lordships View and Favourable acceptance, such Collections and Observations (which I here humbly offer) as I had made thereupon; and so much the rather I was induced thereunto, because of Your Lordships respect to Antiquities, so signally manifested in Patronizing, with your Purse and Countenance, that our notable English Antiquary, Mr. Roger Dodsworth, in his Collections, composing and publishing of that singular Piece his Monasticon, which with indefatigable diligence he hath recovered and brought to light, out of the Bowells (as it were) of devouring Time. Good Lawes enlivened in a due execution of them, are so beneficiall to

Mankind in the conservation of humane Society, as that the Law-givers and Administrators of such, have been ever had, even with the most barbarous Nations, in very great veneration; and therefore although Supream Offices in Government are in order to publique Good, things lawfully desireable, and may be endeavour'd after in a just way, by persons fitly qualified for them; but for that few have been found to have managed such Powers well, sollicitations of this sort are, for the most part, attended with strong prejudices; Whence it is, that Persons of most merit, least seeking, and readiliest laying down, places of the highest Trust and Importance in a Common-Wealth; have been held the fittest to possesse them: A rare Example whereof your Lordship stands evidenc'd to the whole World: And it is well known also, that your Lordship became vested in this Seigniorie of Man towards the acknowledgment of a publique Gratitude for your high Deserts; and that it was not the Issue of your own Desires: By this means, there is put into your hands the exercising of a Legislative, as well as Ministeriall Power in an eminent degree; which doubtlesse your Lordships well grounded principles of Religion and Honour will lead forth into Pious and Honourable Actings; which, my prayers are, may be crowned with prosperous Successes. And so humbly taking my leave, I remain devoted,

My Lord,

Your most humble Servant,

Middle-Park,
   Decemb. 1, 1653.   JAMES CHALONER[2]

THE ISLAND DESCRIBED.

————————

CHAPTER I.

CONCERNING THE
SCITUATION OF THE ISLE OP MAN.

————————

A S Ireland, anciently, was styled Brittain the lesse, in relation to England and Scotland, then called Brittain the Great; so this Island was stiled Monoeda, or the Remoter Man, by the Brittish; and Manea by the Latines, to distinguish How call'd.
it from Mona, now Anglesey: but since Anglesey hath lost her ancient name, in our Speech; this Island hath assumed the Name of Mona, or Man, without any difference: yet the Inhabitants in their Speech call it Maning.[3]

This Island is scituated in that part of the Brittish Sea, that is called St. Georg's Channel, which lyeth between The contents.
England and Ireland: It containeth, in length, about thirty miles;[4] that is to say, from the Point of Ayr in the North, to the Isle of the Calf in the South; and, in breadth, in some places more, in some lesse; the broadest not exceeding nine miles; the narrowest not lesse then five. It is, generally, a The natural
high Land upon the Sea-coast, defended likewise with strength.
Rocks, lying out as far, if not further, into the Sea, then the Low-water Mark: yet upon the Eastern Sea, in the North part of the Isle, it is a bold Coast and Beach upon the shore; and in the South-East part some Low-land, but that inaccessible with shipping, in regard the Coast is so perillous with Rocks. The Harbours for shipping are The Harbours.
Douglas, the safest, then Rainsway,[5] then Ramsey; and

Laxie the meanest, these looking towards England; and the Peel, a poor Harbour, facing Ireland: but let the wind blow where, or how it will, there will be in one quarter of the Isle, or other, a Lee-shore,[6] where ships may ride with some safety; but in no Season of the year is this Narrow Channell safe for great ships to abide in, there being no Harbours to receive them, either upon this, or the English Coast.[7]

A dangerous Coast.

This Island, even to wonder, in so small a Tract of Land, abounds in Springs of water; by which means it is supplyed with divers usefull and pleasant Rivolets. The Soyl is indifferently fertile, yet it is conceived, that two parts of three are Mountains[8] (which from the Eastern to the Western Coast, cross the middest of the Isle) the most eminent of which, are Maroun and Cubgreve;[9] but Snawfell[10] surmounteth all the rest. It yieldeth Rye, Wheat, and Barley, but chiefly Oats, the ordinary Breadcorn of the Inhabitants. It is stored with Beasts, Sheep, bearing a coorse fleece; some of which are called Lawton-sheep,[11] bearing a sort of Wooll; which, without dying, maketh a kind of Sand-colour'd cloth; also, with Goats and Horses, but all of a small size. The Seas afford no plenty of Fish, or rather the People (though many of them use the Sea for that purpose) know not how to take them, but of Herrings[12] onely, which come upon the Coast towards the end of August in shoals, and continue there in their passage the space of a moneth, or thereabouts.

Of Fowl, this Island hath plenty, and great variety, especially in the Isle of the Calf; where there is a sort of Sea-Fowl, called Puffines,[18] of a very unctuous Constitution, which breed in the Coney-holes, (the Conies leaving their Burrows for that time) are never seen with their Young, but either very early in the morning, or late in the evening; nourishing (as is conceived) their Young with Oyl; which drawn from their own Constitution, is dropped into their mouths; for that being opened, there is found in their Crops no other sustenance but a single Sorrel-leaf, which the Old give their Young, for digestions sake, as is conjectured; the flesh of these Birds is nothing pleasant fresh, because of their rank and Fish-like taste; but, pickled or salted, they may be ranked with Anchoves, Caviare, or the like; but profitable they are in their feathers, and Oyl, of which they make great use about their Wooll. Here are some Ayries of mettled Faulcons, that build in the Rocks, great store of Conies, Red-deer; and in the Summer time, there arrive here out of Ireland, and the Western parts of Scotland, many of those small Hawks, called Merlyns.

It is apparent, though it be now destitute of Wood, it hath had great plenty; witnesse the Oaks digged up often from under ground;[14] and the certainty that it would yet grow there, if planted, is proved by the Plantations, which some few have made about their houses, as well of Fruit-trees, as others: Yet is not this Countrey destitute of Fewel, for it affordeth great plenty of Turf and Pete; and, of Pete, the best that ever I saw; which, though not so durable as Cole, yet is it lasting, and more pleasant in the burning.

Lime stone.

There is Lyme-stone in the South part of the Isle; but no Quarries of Free-stone any where, but upon the Sea-side, neer Balladouly; but that very difficult to be polish'd, in regard of the hardnesse thereof: of which stone, Castle-Rushen, hereafter mentioned, was built.[15] No sort of Minerals have been here found, but Ore of Lead, at, and neer unto the Sea-Crag, called Mine-hough, which hath been experimented by Captain Edward Christian[16] (who was employed in Command at Sea by the East-Indy Company; and sometimes under King James, in one of his Royall Ships; sometime also Lieutenant of this Isle; then Receiver; and lastly, Major Generall; a Native of this Countrey, and of the principal Family there) to hold much Silver; the Veins of this Mine, by it's brightnesse, may plainly be discerned in the

Free stone.

Lead.

Rock towards the Sea; but it seemeth not possible to be wrought, in regard the Sea beats upon it constantly at High-water, unlesse it may be done by Mining within the Land; a tryall whereof were worth the undertaking, in regard of the great benefit that possibly may ensue thereof.[17]

To conclude, the Air is quick and healthfull, Frosts short and seldome; Snow in the Valleys, by reason of its Vicinity to the Sea, will soon dissolve; and subject it is to extraordinary high Winds.[18]

CHAPTER II.

CONCERNING THE INHABITANTS.

———————

DOUBTLESSE this Island was first peopled from the Hebrides, or Highlands of Scotland, their Language being the very same with that of the Scottish-Irish; which is the same with that of Ireland; though spoken in a different Dialect: yet as the Isle is named Man; so are the People styled Manks-men, and their Speech, Manks; And although[19] the same hath great affinity with the Welsh or Brittish, (which that singularly Learned, Hospitable, painfull, and pious Prelate, Doctor Philips, late Bishop of Man, and a Native of North-Wales, well experimented; who out of Zeal, to the propagating of the Gospel in these parts, attained the knowledge thereof so exactly, that he did ordinarily preach in it, and undertook that most laborious, most difficult but most useful Work, of the Translation of the Bible into Manks, taking to his assistance some of the Islanders; as namely. Sir[20] Hugh Cavoll,[21] Minister of the Gospel, and now Vicar of Kirk-Michael, perfected the said Work in the space of twenty and nine years) yet he observed he could not have been able to have gone through with it, but for the helps he found in his own Native Tongue; and no marvell, since that the People of Ireland are descended of the Brittains.

It is worth the observing, that many of their derivation of words are derived from the Latine and Greek,[22] and some are of pure English; such words, for the most part, signifie things Forraign, and which originally were not known to them, or in use amongst them. It also may be observed, that they put the Noun-substantive, always before the Adjective; as. Horse-white, Cow-black, &c.

Peopled by Scottish-Irish.

Bible translated.

The derivation of some words

But it may be enquired, how came these mixtures of Languages?

It is more then probable, that as their speech at first (as of all other Nations) consisted of few, but significant words, suitable to the simplicity of their Manners; so, in processe of time, by their conversation with Strangers, alteration of Manners, Forraign Merchandize, and new Inventions, came to be introduced, which necessitated them to an enlargment of their speech: But finding it more easie to take the words of such by whom they were introduced, then to coyn new of their own, these Mixtures of Languages have in all likelyhood been produced. Few speak the English Tongue.[28]

The Inhabitants of ancient time were, doubtlesse, as all the Neighbouring Tract, very rude and barbarous; untill by the planting of Christianity amongst them, (as in the next Chapter you shall understand) they came to be reformed:

mixing with the English, they are at this day a very civill People, laborious, contented with simple Diet and lodging; their Drink, water; their Meat, Fish; their Bedding, Hay or Straw, generally; much addicted to the Musick of the Violyne; so that there is scarce a Family in the Island, but more or lesse can play upon it; but as they are ill Composers, so are they as bad Players; and it is strange they should be singular in affecting this Instrument before others, their Neighbours; the Northern English, the Scots, the Highlanders, and the Irish, generally, affecting the Bag-Pipe: they are ingenuous, in learning of Manufactures, and apt for the Studies of Humanity or Divinity, bearing a great esteem and reverence to the Publique service of God; which they testifie by their seldome absenting themselves from the Church, although sometime a great distance from it; yet are they given to Incontinencie of body, which naturally may be imputed to their eating so much Fish; which is of a flatuous nature.

CHAPTER III.

OF THE STATE ECCLESASTICALL.

———

SAINT Patrick, by Nation a Brittain, born in the year of our Lord God, 372, in the utmost limits of the Roman Province in Brittain, between the City of Glascow and Dunbarton-Castle, at a place called Kirk-Patrick, or Kill-Patrick; his Parents Calphurinus a Deacon, who was the son of Potitus a Presbyter; his Mother Conca of Pannonia, now Austria and Hungarie, and Sister to St Martin the renowned Bishop of Tours. He was educated in the study of the holy Scriptures, within his own Countrey; but by travelling into the parts beyond the Seas, he much encreased in the knowledge thereof; for there he was a disciple to his Uncle St. Martyn, who conferr'd Sacerdoticall Orders upon him; as also to St. Germane, Bishop of Auxerre; and by Amator the immediate predecessour of St. Germane, in that See made a Bishop, and by him named Magonius; whereas in his Christendome his name was Suchat: He travell'd through all Italy, abiding at Home a long time; where he became a Canon of Lateran; by which means he became also very expert in the Roman Tongue, in Ecclesiastical Government and regular Discipline: By Pope Caelestine he was constituted the Apostle and Metropolitane of Ireland, and by him nam'd Patricius; having for his assistants in that sacred Expedition, Secundinus, Auxilius and Iservinus, Canons of Lateran; by his constant preaching, his frequency in prayer, watchings and Fasts often; by the holinesse of his life, and the blessing of God upon his pious endeavours, and happy successe in converting the Irish to the Faith, entitled by way of Excellency, Saint Patrick.

Beholden to Jac. Ussensus Armach. Arch. Ang. Ecc. Br.

Stiria and Carinthia.

This St. Patrick, in or about the year of our Lord God 432, arriving in Ireland, and finding the Harvest great, and the Labourers few, he returned into Brittain for more help; and returning again for Ireland with a purpose to convert this and the other Islands to the Faith, in his passage thither, he came ashore in this Isle, converted it to the Faith, and placed a Bishop there;[24] namely, Germanus his Disciple, a Canon of Lateran, a holy and wise man; introducing withall the Liturgie of Lateran, composed by Mark the Evangelist; erecting his Episcopal Seat in Patrick's Isle, (now Peele-Castle) because St. Patrick had for some time there made his abode; and this was in the year 447, and that was (be it for the honour of this Isle now remembred) 150 years at the least before the Conversion of the English Saxons: Next by the appointment of St Patrick succeeded Conindrus or Connidrius, and Romulus, fellow-Bishops, in whose time there arrived in this Isle one Macfil, alias Maguil or Machalilus;[25] who in a Leathern Boat putting to Sea, and endeavouring Northward, fortuned to be cast upon this Isle; the said Bishops receiving him with admiration and pity, both in regard of the hazards he had run at Sea, as for the strangenesse of his habit; and instructed him in the faith; who excelling in piety, succeeded the said Bishops in this Isle, and built a Town therein, which beareth his name (as hereafter shall be remembred) to this day. And this I find of their Conversion, and of the ancient Bishops.[26] In after-times this Island, and the Hebrides or Western Iles of Scotland, being possess'd by the Norwegians, there was but one Bishop of this and the said Isles, who was stiled Bishop of Man or Sodor, from a Village call'd Sodor in St. Columb's Isle, where anciently there had been a Bishops Seat for that and the rest of the Western Isles;[27] the first of which was Wermundus alias Wimundus; who for his cruelty was banish'd the Isle, and had his eyes put out;[28] then began they to be

The Manks Converted.

Germanus the first Bishop.

Conindrus and Romulus

Machaldus.

consecrated by the Metropolitane of Norway, that is, of Trondheim; before, by the Archbishops of York; because it lay nearer to England then to Ireland, and had belonged thereto in ancient time: After Wermundus, succeeded John, a Monk of Sais.[29] And in the year 1247, one Symon sate Bishop, who departed this life at Kirk-Michael; in which Parish now is, and it seemeth then was, the Bishops Pallace, call'd Bishops Court; he was buried in St. Patrick's Isle in the Church of St. Germane, the Cathedrall Church of this Isle, which he began to build: And this Isle and the rest coming under the subjection of the Scots in 1266, Scotland then wanting Archbishops, the Bishop did receive confirmation and consecration in Norway.[30]

In the year 1348, William Russell, a Native, and Abbot of St Mary of Rushin, was elected Bishop by the Clergie, who resorting to Pope Clement the 6th at Avignion, was the first Bishop that was consecrated and confirmed by the Pope.[31]

In our Times, there have sate two Bishops very eminent for Piety and Learning; The first was Dr. Philips,[32] a Native of Wales; educated in Oxford, Dr. Philips, who out of zeal to the propagating of the Gospel, attained the Manks Tongue, and did not onely preach in it, but translated the Bible into it, (as before hath been remembred) which by his death never came to the Presse; so that the Ministers read the Scriptures to the people in the Manks, out of the English; The other was Dr. Parr, (33) a Lancashire man, sometime Fellow of Brasen-nose Colledge in Oxford, who whilest he continued in the University, was very painfull to my own knowledge, being my self of the same Colledge, in reading the Arts to young Schollers; and afterwards having cure of Souls, no lesse industrious in the Ministry.

And here it may be observed, that after this Isle came to be possessed by the English, this Bishoprick was divided into two: the one of this place, who retained still his name of

Dr. Philips, Bishop.

Dr. Parr Bishop.

Bishop of Man or Sodor; the other of the Isles, whose seat was in Jona or St. Columb's Isle; this, belonging to the See of York; the other, to that of Glascow.

Bishops made
by the Lords.

The Bishops in our time have been elected by the Lords of the Isle, without whose confirmation the Leases made by the Bishops were not valid in Law; they were in the quality of their chiefest Barons; the Bishops ordering matters Ecclesiasticall with the suffrage of the Archdeacon and Vicar-General; for the substance in such manner as hath been used in England.

Bishops Barons
of Man.

There was anciently a multiplicity of Chappels[34] in this Isle; which generally in all other places as well as here, were the Originals of Parish Churches; which are now in number 17, namely, Kirk-Christ-Rushen, Mr. Thomson[35] an English man, Minister, sometime Schoolmaster at Castleton, so called, because built on the side of a Rushy bog.[36] Kirk-Arborie, because formerly surrounded with Trees Arbour-like, Sir John Crelling[37] Minister; and here observe once for all, that the Ministers who are Natives, have alwaies this Addition of Sir, unless they be Parsons of their Parish (of which there are but few; most of the Parsonages being impropriate to the Lord of the Isle or Bishop) and then instead of Sir, they have the Addition of Parson. Kirk-Malew, because dedicated to St. Malew, Sir Thomas Parr[38] Minister. Kirk-Santon, because dedicated to St. Anne, void, because of the displacing of old Sir John Coshenham.[33] Kirk-Bradan; Bradan in Manks signifieth a Salmon; and that Church hath that name, either because it is built by the Salmon River, or because dedicated to a Saint of that name; why may it not be so named from one of the Bishops, Brocadius or Brachanus the sons of Tigris, St Patricks sister, Sir Patrick Thomson, Minister. Kirk-Concan, because dedicated to Conca, the Mother of St. Patrick, Sir John Woods Minister. Kirk-Lomman, because dedicated to Lomanus, another of the sons

of Tigris, and the first Bishop of Trim in Ireland, Sir James
More Minister. Kirke Maughold to Maughold, being Bishop
here. as is before remembred. Sir Robert Allen Minister.
Kirk-Maroune to that Saint, Sir William Oates Minister.
Kirke Patrick of Peel, because within the Castle of the Peel,
and dedicated to St. Patrick, Sir Thomas Harrison Minister.
Kirk-Germane, to that Saint, being the first Bishop here, also
within the said castle. Sir William Coshenham[40] Minister.
Kirk-Michael to St Michael the Archangell, Sir Hugh
Cannell, Minister, assistant to Bishop Philips in translating
of the Bible. Saint Mary of Ballaugh, so called, because
dedicated to St. Mary: Ballaugh signifies in Manks, Mire-
town, because it is situated in a place, that formerly was a
bog, Mr. Robert Parr,[41] Parson, to whom I was beholden for
some derivation of places. Kirk-Patrick of Jurby; this Church
was dedicated to St. Patrick; and to distinguish it from Kirk-
Patrick of Peel, it is called St. Patrick of Jurby; and Jurby is
the name of that Land, whereon it is erected. Sir William
Crow Minister. Kirk-Andrew, because dedicated to St
Andrew, Sir John Huddlestone[42] the present Curate. This
Parsonage belong'd alwaies to the Archdeacon. Kirk Bride,
because dedicated to St Bridget, who received the Vail of
Virginity of St Patrick, or from some of his disciples, when
she was not full 14 years of age; a Virgin highly remarked in
her time for sanctity; and born in the province of Ulster, and
Abbesse of a Cell within the city of Killdare, Mr. John
Harrison, Parson. Kirk-Christ le Ayre, called le Ayre, to
distinguish it from Kirk Christ-Rushen, and because it is
placed in a sharp Ayr; Sir Edward Crow,[43] Minister.

There have been three Monasteries in this Isle, the chiefest   Monasteries.
of which was the Priory of Rushen,[44] which sprang out of
that of Furnesse in Lancashire, founded 1134, by King Olaus
the first of that name, who endowed it with considerable
Rents and Liberties; the Fabrick of which by the ruines there-

The Prospect of ... Abbey on the ...
South West side.

The Prospect of the Nunry in y.e Ille of Man on the East side.

The Prospect of Bishops Court in the Isle of Man on the Garden

of, appeareth to have been none of the meanest; and which was the Sepulture of their Kings. There was also the Priory of Douglas, and a house of the Friers-minors at Bimaken,[45]

Now that Episcopacy, with the Ecclesiasticall Jurisdiction accompanying the same, is put down in England, the same is also by their example laid here aside; and the Bishops Lands and Jurisdictions are thereupon devolved to the Lord of the Isle; who for the better encouragement and support of the Ministers of the Gospel, and for the promoting of Learning, hath conferr'd all this revenue upon the Ministers;[46] as also for the maintaining of Free-Schooles *i.e.* Free-Schools. at Castletown, Peel, Douglas, and Ramsey; and considering the Ministers here are generally Natives, and have had their whole education in the Isle, it is marvailous to hear what good Preachers there be; and truly, for about 50 or 60 years last past, their Bishops have been persons of singular piety,[47] frequent Preachers, excellent Patterns for the Clergie under them to take out by.

The proving of Wills,[48] prophanation of the Lords Day, Drunkennesse, swearing, Incontinencie and the like, are to fall under the Cognisance of the Civill Magistrate.

The Devotion of the Kings of this Isle was extended beyond their own Jurisdictions; insomuch, that they had conferred Tithes or lands in this Isle upon severall Monasteries without the bounds thereof (i.) upon the Priory of St. Bees, or de Sancta Bega in Cumberland; (ii.) upon the Abby of Whittern in Scotland, sometime the Episcopal Seat of St. Ninianus; and (iii.) upon the Abby of Banchor in Ireland. For this cause the Prior and Abbots of these Houses were Barons of Man, and were obliged to give their attendance as such, upon the Kings and Lords thereof, whensoever they should require it; or at the least upon every new succession in the Government, upon the penalty of forfeiting their said respective Interests.[49]

CHAPTER IV.

OF THE CIVILL GOVERNMENT.

———————

THIS Island (as before is said) being first of all inhabited by the ancient Scots;[50] that is to say, by the Irish or Highlanders of Scotland; so doubtlesse had they Governours of their own Nation, of whom I find mention to be made onely of Two.

First of one Mananan Mac Bar[51] a Pagan and Necromancer, who by raising of storms and mists, is said to secure himself in that Government from forrain invasion; or rather by the natural situation of the place, subject to storms and mists; who took of the people no other acknowledgment for their land, but the bearing of Rushes to certain places call'd Warefield, and Mame, on Midsummer even.

The other was named Birle, of whom besides his name, I find nothing recorded.

This Island hath also sometime belong'd to Brittain. It is not extant in any History that I have met with, that this Island was ever under the Jurisdiction of the Romans; for by Mona in Caesar[52] and Tacitus, is to be understood Anglesey; but that it was under the awe (which, as their fame, was diffused every where) of their Empire, no question is to be made; especially since it lay even within the prospect of Brittain; yet by the Urns there found, the contrary would seem to be apparent; some enclosed in Coffins[53] of stone; one Coffin containing divers of them: and in such sort Dr. Batthurst, skillfull in Antiquities, and a carefull, learned, and judicious Physician of London hath observed them to be found in the Northern parts of England, about Featherstone-haugh; and near Bishops-Court: Whilest I remained in this Island, I caused one of those round hills (which in the Plains of Wiltshire are very frequent, and by the Inhabitants termed Barrowes, like as in the Midland parts of England they call them Lowes commonly and truly held to be the Sepultures of the Danes or Norwegians, and others of that Northern tract invading and possessing Brittain) to be opened; in which were found 14 rotten Urns, or earthen pots, placed with their mouths downwards; and one more neatly then the rest in a bed of fine white sand, containing nothing but a few brittle bones, (as having pass'd the fire) no ashes left discernable: hereabouts are divers of these Hills to be seen; but in other parts of the Isle, few and dispersedly; some of these being environ'd with great stones pitched endwayes in the earth: This Countrey was possessed (as presently will appear) by the Norwegians; whose rite of Buriall was in ancient time (as all the Northern people in that Tract, if eminent persons) to burn the bodies of their dead; and to preserve within the earth in vessels of glasse, earth or stone their ashes; and this was introduc'd or establish'd by a Law, by Othinus their King, and continued among them and the Swedes longer then with the rest; as Olaus Wormius, publique Professor of Physick in the University of Haffen, the same is it which by the Germans is called Copenhagen, in his Learned Danish Antiquities hath well inform'd me; by the testimony of good Authors, and Experience itself; whose discourse giveth better light (writing but of his own Countrey) to the knowledge of divers ancient Monuments among us, then doth appear from our own Historians, evincing not onely vulgar errours of this kind; but the Judicious will be hereby the better able to difference Roman Antiquities from Saxon, and the like; wherein without much consideration, it is easie to mistake; as among us by common experience we find. But pardon this somewhat of digression.

Afterwards It came under the subjection of Edwine K. of

Northumberland; which being all that I read of it, I conceive
that either he or his Successours soon deserted it; or were
expulsed thence.[54]

In the year 1066, it came under the subjection of the
Norwegians by Conquest,[55] and so did shortly after the
Hebrides or Western Isles of Scotland; by which means the
Kings of Man were stiled the Kings of Man, and of the Isles;
of this race there were 12 in number: 1. Godred, sirnamed
Crovan, the son of Harald the black of Izland. 2. Lagman, the
eldest son of Crovan. 3. Magnus, King of Norway. 4. Olauus
the son of Godred Crovan. 5. Godred his son. Reginald the
6th King, base brother to Godred. 7. Reginald, base son to
Godred. 8. Olauus the legitimate son of Godred, 9. Harald
his son. 10. Reginald his brother. 11. Harald the son of
Godred Don. 12. Magnus and last King of Man of the
Norwegian race, who dyed in the year 1265; so that this
Government had continuance 199 years, together with a
constant succession of calamities both domestique and from
abroad, which for the readers information, I desire leave to
refer him to Mr. Camden's *Britannia*.

Then the dominion of this Isle and the Western Islands
was translated to Alexander K. of Scots, partly by force and
partly by agreement with the K. of Norway to whom and his
successours, he was to pay 3 marks in Gold upon every new
accession to the Crown. This Isle the Scots[56] held but 74
years, but the Western Isles even to our times.[57]

Mary[58] the daughter of Reginald the last K. of Man of
that name, next heir to the Crown, married to the Earl of
Strathern in Scotland, complained to Edw: the first King of
England at St. John's Town, at such time as he invaded
Scotland, for her right, but without remedy; whereupon John
de Waldebeofe her Grandchild in the 33 year of the same
Kings raign, made his request to the Parliament; but getting
no redresse neither; William Mountacute Knight, deriving

an Interest in blood from the said Mary, took this Isle by force of Arms from the Scots, but by reason of the great charge he was at in subduing it, he was constrained to mortgage it to Anthony Bec Bishop of Duresme, and Patriarch of Jerusalem for the space of 7 years.

The said Bishop of Duresme had it by Grant of the K. afterwards during his life.

Pierce Gaveston that voluptuous insolent and ambitious Gascoyn, and the Bane of his Soveraign Edw. 2d. to whom he was Favourite, by grant from the said King had it conferr'd upon him what time as he created him Earl of Cornwall.

The said King gave it after he was beheaded, to Henry Lord Beaumont,[59] who was devested of the same, as by the Record appears.

Charta[60] *Edwardi II. Regis Angliae, Insulam de Man concedens Henrico de Bello-Monte, pro vitâ, Cujus Recordatio rediviva & in lucem revocata effulsit, ab elucubratis & insopitis studiis viri verè proenobilis, Antiquitatis indagatoris indefessi, & perpetuis proeconiis in posteros ebuccinandi, &c.*
Domini Wingfeldi Bodenham Equitis Aurati.

INSULA DE MAN, DATA HENRICO DE BELLO-MONTE,[61]
PRO VITA.

REX omnibus ad quos, &c. salutem. Sciatis quod pro bono servitio quod dilectus consanguineus, et fidelis noster Henricus de Bello-Monte nobis hactenus impendit, dedimus ei et concessimus pro nobis et haeredibus nostris, totam terrain nostram de Man, habendam et tenendam eidem Henrico ad totam vitam suam de nobis et haeredibus

1 Ed II.

nostris, libere, quiete, bene, integre, et in pacecum omni Dominio et Justitia Regali, una cum feodis militum, Advocationibus Ecclesiarum, et domorum Religiosaram, libertatibus, liberis consuetudinibus, escaetis, et omnibus aliis ad praedictam terram spectantibus, seu spectare volentibus, quoquo modo per servitia quae Domini terrae predictae Regibus Scotiae inde facere consueverant. In cujus rei, &c. Teste Rege apud Novum-Castrum super Tynam, primo die Maii, per ipsum Regem.

EX ROTULO PATENT DE AN. 5. E. 2. M. 3.

Ed. II. AUSSINT pur ceo q̃ mons' Henri de Beaumont ad pris 6 de nr̃e Seign' le Roi, au damage et deshonur du Roi puis le temps de l'ordeinement des Ordeinours a quel le Roi se agrea, le Roiaume de Man et autres terres, rentes, franchises, et baillies et procure de doner as autres terres, et tenementz, fraunchises, et bailliers countre cel ordeinement, et pur ceo q'il ad malcounseillez le Roi encontre son serment, nous ordeinons q'il soit oustez du Counseil le Roi pur touz jour, et q̃ pres du Roi mesne viegne nule part s'il ne soit, a commune somounse du Parlement, ou en guerre si le Roi le voet avoir s'il ne soit p commun assent des Ercevesqes, Evesqes, Countes, et Barouns, et ceo en plain Parlement; et totes les autres terres q'il tient dedeinz le Roiaume D'engleterre soient pris en la meyn le Roi D'engleterre, et tenues taunt q̃ le Roi, eit receuz des issues de celes terres, la value de touz lez esplez q̃ le dit Sire Henri ad pris des terres receuez countre le dit ordeinement. Et si l'avant dit Sire Henri viegne en nul point countre ceste ordeinance, soit desheritez pur touz jours de touz lez terres q'il aden Engleterre du doun le Roi.

Pur ceo q̃ trove ost par examinement des Prelatz, Countes,

et Barons, q̃ la Dame de Vescy, ad procure le Roi, a doner a Sire Henri de Beaumount son frere, et as autres, terres, fraunchises, et baillies au damage et deshonur du Roi, et apte desheriteson de la Corone, et ausint procure de maunder hors lettres de souz la targe contre lei, et l'ententioun du Roi; Nous ordeinons, q̃ ele aile a sa meson, et ceo dedeinz la quinzeine de Seint Michiel prechien a venir saunz james returner a la Court pur demore faire, et que pur toutes cestez choses avant dites. Et q̃ pur toutes cestes choses avant dites, et pur ceo q̃ hom̃e entent q̃ le Chaustel de Baunburgh est de la Corone, Nous ordeinons aussint, q̃ cel Chaustel soit repris de lui, en la mein le Roi, et q̃ mes ne soit baillee a li ne a autre forsq̃ a la volunte le Roi.

DE HENRICO DE BELLO-MONTE PROPTER INOBEDIENTAM SUAM ERGA REGEM PRISONAE COMMISSO.

16 Ed. II. D OMINUS noster Rex existens apud Bishopthorp juxta Eboracum tricessimo die Maii, Anno Regni sui sexto decimo, vocari fecit coram ipso, ad Concilium suum ibidem, venerabiles patres Willielmum Archepiscopum Eboraci Angliae primatum; J. Norwiciensem Episcopnm, Cancell- arium suum; W. Exoniensem Episcopum, Thesaurarium suum: Edmundum Comitem Kanciae, fratrem suum; Adomarum de Valencia, Comitem Pembrokiae; Hugonem le Despenser, Comitem Winton. David de Strobolgy Comitem Athol. Hugonem le Despenser juniorem, Willielmum le Ros de Hamelake, et plures alios Barones, et nobiles de regno suo, ac Justiciarios suos de utroque Banco, Barones de Scaccario et alios de consilio suo, ad tractandum super quadam Treuga inter ipsum Dominum Regem et Robertum de Brus, suosque complices, et fautores, contra Dominum Regem de guerra existentes, prelocuta, firmanda, vel neganda, inter quos

nobiles Dominus Henricus de Bellomonte, Baro, et de Magno et Secreto Concilio ipsius Domini Regis juratus, vocatus fuit, et ibidem venit; et cum dictus Dominus noster Rex, volens scire consilium et avisamentum omnium ibidem coram ipso ex causa praedicta existentium, et cujuslibet eorum singulariter, super negotiis praedictis, et inter caeteros plures ore proprio injunxisset dicto Henrico, et ipsum requisivisset, ut eidem Domino Regi consuleret in hac parte, dictus Henricus quodam motu excessivo, et animo quasi irreverenti, Dicto domino Regi, saepiùs respondit, quod sibi consulere noluit in hac parte: De qua responsione, idem dominus Rex commotus, praecepit dicto Henrico, quod Consilium suum exiret, et idem Henricus exeundo Concilium, dixit, modo quo priùs, et quod plus sibi placeret á dicto Concilio absentari, quám eidem interesse; Super quibus idem Dominus Rex praefatis magnatibus et aliis de Concilio suo ibidem existentibus, praecepit, quod consulerent de Judicio faciendo, de dicto Henrico in hac parte, sicut idem Henricus homo suus ligius et Baro, ac de Concilio suo secreto juratus fuit, et requisitus de consulendo dicto domino Regi, super tanto, et tam arduo negotio, ipsum Dominum Regem, et regnum suum ita specialiter tangente, eidem sic respondit quod eidem Domino regi consulere noluit, et alia opprobria dixit, sicut praedictum est, et quod judicium illud facerent: Et habito inde per dictos magnates et alios de Concilio Domini Regis ibidem existentes, tractatu, et deliberatione diligenti, praefatoque Henrico coram dicto Domino Rege magnatibus et aliis supradictis, ibidem eodem die postmodum revocato, consideratum est per praedictos Magnates, et alios de Concilio supradicto, quod dictus Henricus committatur prisonsae, pro contemptu et inobedientia supradictis. Et postea Henricus de Percy, Radulfus de Nevill, Simon Warde, Henricus filius Hugonis, Rogerus de Sommervill, et Thomas Ugthred de Comitatu

Eboraci, et Willielmus Ridell, et Thomas Gray de Comitatu
Northumbriae manuceperunt praedictum Henricum de
Bello-monte videlicet quilibet eorum, corpus pro corpore
habendum coram Domino rege in eodem statu quo nunc est
cum inde fuerint praemoniti.

****

The Scots recovered it under Robert Brus; and then that
couragious Scot, Robert Randulph enjoy'd it. Alexander,
Duke of Albanie, second son to James the 2d. of Scotland,
bare the empty Title and Arms of Man, but had not the
Seigniory; for William Mountacute the younger, E. of
Salisbury, in the year 1340, won it from the Scots.

Will. M. E. of
Salisbury, Lord.

Then William Mountacute son of the said William, and
Earl of Salisbury possess'd the same.

1393, Sir Will.
Scroop, Lord.

E. of North.
Lord

Then in the year 1393, by purchase it came into the hands
of Sir William Scroop, who being attainted of High Treason
by H. the 4th, the K. disposed it to H. Piercy E. of Northumberland, with this Tenure, That he should carry the Sword
of Lancaster on the Coronation day; but soon after he
forfeited the same by Treason also, and then the K. conferr'd
it upon Sir John Stanley Treasurer of his houshold, in the year

1403. The
Stanleys Lords.

1403. whose posterities were afterwards Earls of Derby, and
held it by presenting a cast of Faulcons[62] to the K. on the
Coronation day, unto these our times, when James the last
Earl, for bearing Arms against the Parliament, was attainted
of high Treason by a Councell of War, and his Estate
confiscated by Act of Parliament, losing his head at Bolton:
And lastly, this Isle by Authority of Parliament was devolved

1649. Thomas
Lord Fairfax
Lord of Man
and the Isles

to Thomas Lord Fairfax, in as large and beneficiall manner
to all intents and purposes, as the said James had, or might
have enjoyed the same, towards the acknowledgment of his

great services performed in the Office of Captain Generall of all the Parliaments Forces, which he so honourably had undergone; so that as his Lordship hath the Jurisdiction of the Isle, as the said Earl had; so hath he also the Title, namely, Lord of Man, and of the Isles: and that most deservedly; for that as He in vertue and Nobility of Blood is not inferiour to any of his Predecessours, Kings or Lords of Man; so in high Archievements in Arms he far surmounteth them all.[63]

And thus having given account of the Supream Governours of the Isle, I shall descend to the inferiour Officers and the Judicatories thereof as they are at this day; for which I am beholden to Mr. Tynslie the Lord's Atturney General, very expert in the Laws.

This Government is ordered by and under a Lievtenant or Governour, Major Wade, with the assistance of two Deemsters or Judges, John Christian[64] and William Qualtrough; for matters of Law; And of Henry Sharplesse, Controller, and Clerk of the Rolls; William Christian, Receiver;[65] Hugh Moor, Water-Bailiffe; and Robert Tynsley Atturney-Generall.[66]

To whose Assistance in cases of doubt, and considerations sometimes taken about the ordering of the affairs of the Country, for the defence and safety thereof; and propositions of good and wholesome Lawes and Orders, for the Peace and Welfare of the People, in matters of Right betwixt the Lord and the People, and betwixt party and party; the said Governour and Officers do usually call the 24 Keyes of the Island, especially once every year, viz. upon Midsummer day, at St John's Chappel, to the Tinewald Court there, where upon a Hill near unto the said Chappel, all the Inhabitants of the Island, standing round about a fair Plain, they may hear the Laws and Ordinances agreed upon before in the Chappel aforesaid, published and declar'd unto them, and then, and there, the Lord of the Island, if he be in the

Countrey, is to Sit in a Chair of State, covered with a Royal
Cloth or Canopy over his head; his visage into the East, with
his sword before him holden, with the point upward: His
Barons, viz. the Bishops and Abbots when was time, with the
rest in their degrees, sitting beside him; his beneficed men,
or fee'd Council, and Deemesters, sitting before him; his
Gentry and Yeomanry in the third degree, and the 24 Keys
aforesaid in their Order; and the Commons to stand without
the Circle, with three Clerks in their Surplices.

6 Coroners or
Sheriffs of the 6
Sheadings into
which the Isle is
divided.
Then the Deemster calls the Coroner of Glanfaba, who is
the chief Coroner of the Land, and commands him to fence
Court; which is, that no man make any disturbance or tumult
in the time of the Tynwald, or any murmure, or rising, upon
pain of hanging and drawing. After this, the said Coroner of
Glanfaba calls in the other five Coroners; and he, and all of
them, upon their knees, deliver the Rods of their Offices into
the Lords hand, if he be present; and then his Lordship calls
six other men of the six Sheadings, and delivers every of them
one of the said Rods; and there upon their knees, they take
their Oaths, for the due execution of their places; which the
eldest Deemster administers to them in the Manks Tongue.
After this order, the Governour proceeds every year in his
Lordships absence upon Midsummer day: And if any Orders
be agreed upon by the Officers, and 24 Keys, they are to be
presented to the Lord of the Island, as from that Court; and
if his Lordship like well of, and please to confirm them, they
are retmned back, and put upon Record; and at the next
Tynwald, after, proclaimed for absolute Laws.

This Country is very happy in the ready and easie Trials
of their Rights, upon little or no charge, as followeth:

The Governour twice in the year, *viz*, a week or fortnight
after May; and again, within the like time after Michaelmas
(as he shall please to assigne) calls the Courts for the several
Sheadings (which are in the nature of Court-Leet, and Court-

Baron in England) Of which, the Moors which are the Lords Bayliffs of the Land, give Summons at the Parish-Churches, after Divine Service, the next Sunday before the Courts are to be kept, for such and such Sheadings; and there every man that hath cause of Suits against any of that Sheading, comes to the Moor, and desires him to summon such or such a man, his adverse party, to answer him at the Court. The Moor calls to him two or three of the Parishioners there present, to witnesse with him the summoning of such persons, as shall be named unto him, by the parties who intend to be Plaintiffs at the Court.

At the day assigned by the Governour, as aforesaid, the Deemsters go with him to the place assigned for the keeping of the Courts, which constantly begins at Peel-town, otherwise called Hollam town, neer unto Castle-Peel aforesaid: And at that place, by due Order, there is no Court to be kept, but for the two Parishes of Kirk-Patrick, and Germane, which is called the Sheading of Glanfaba; though now, for more conveniency, the Courts for the two other Sheadings of Kirk-Michael, and Christ-le-Ayr, are also kept in that place; and two days in the week, they sit for the Courts of every Sheading, which spends that week there, beginning upon the Monday.

The next week after, the people having understood of the Courts at Peel for the North side of the Island; the Moors for the South side give their Summons upon the Sunday after, so that the Governour, and Officers, with the Deemsters, are at Douglas upon Monday, for the keeping of the Courts of the Garf-Sheading, which consists of three Parishes, Kirk-Maughall, Lomman, and Conchan; upon Wednesday, or Thursday, they are at Castle-Rushen, and in those two days they end the Court for the Middle-Sheading, which consists of the Parishes of Kirk-Bradan, St. Ann, and Kirk-Marown: And upon the two latter days, Friday and Saturday, for the

Rushen-Court, which consists of the Parishes of Kirk-Malew, Kirk-Arbory, and Kirk-Christ-Rushen; and this is the end of the Sheading-Courts. At these Courts, as they are kept in course aforesaid, the Deemster calls in the chief Moor of the Sheading to Fence-Court: After that a jury of 12 is called, viz. Four, commonly, out of every Parish, who are called the great Inquest for the Sheading; and after they are sworn, the Deemester gives the Charge, as in a Court-Leet in England, (which Jury makes their Presentments at the Head-court, or Court of Goal-delivery at the Half-year). After this Jury sworn, and charge given, as aforesaid, the Moors and Coroners of the Sheading, for which the Court is holden, comes in, and presents, by vertue of their places, what Blood-sheds hath been in the Sheading, since the last Court the half year before: and then four men of every Parish are called and sworn, to find out, and present the bloud-shed; where every man that is found guilty, pays 12*d*. Fine to the Lord, every Woman, for a Man, six pence: besides, for a Woman to the Moor; and for a man, for a Woman, to the Porter of the Castle. And here is the end of that part of the Court, which is called, the Court for the Lords profit, and his Rights of Prerogative, by Fines and Forfeitures: and it is the same with that of the Court-Leet in England; and it is to be remembred, that every one is bound by the Law to appear at this Court, Halt, Lame, and Blind; and thither to come upon a Horse, or Car, upon pain of Fine, as by the Court shall be assessed.

Court-Baron.

Then the Common-Law Courts begin, which are in nature of a Court-Baron. The Plaintiff calls three times to the Deemster, to grant him the Law, which the Deemster grants; and then he tells the matter of his Action, and against whom. The Controller who is Clerk of the Rolls, enters it in form, thus:

A.B. quer. cont. CD. in plt: detent: eo qvod detin. ab eo parcel. ter. de R. &c. unde damnum habet ad valor. &c. Qui appar: &c. And if the Defendant do not appear, as he may by the Law stand out till the third Court, then the Record says, *Qui non app. &c. in misericord. Curioe* 6d. For that is the certain Fine upon any Action whatsoever, be it for small or great value; which the Lord hath upon every non-appearance; and if the Defendant do appear, the Record says, as before, *Qui ap. &c.*

And when all the Actions are enter'd for every Parish in the Sheading, there are four men of every Parish sworn to passe upon the small matters: And after all, a Jury of six, which is called a Sheading Jury, viz. two of every parish, if the Sheading have three Parishes; or three of every Parish, if the Sheading be but two Parishes, as that of Glanfaba is: And this Sheading-Jury passes upon the difficult matters of that Court, for that Sheading; and upon the bringing in of the Verdicts of 4, or 6, as aforesaid; if the Plaintiff recover, the Defendant is in Fine 6*d*.; if he recover nothing, he himself is in 6*d*. Fine, for his unjust complaint: and this is the nature and order of the proceedings in the Court-Baron. Then if any party find himself agrieved with the Verdict of any of these Juries, he comes into the Court, or to the Clerk of the Rolls, at any time after in his Office, and prays, that he may have another Jury to pass upon his businesse, and binds himself in 3*l*. that by the Verdict of that second Jury, he will disprove the Verdict of the former, which had wronged him in their Verdict, as he pretends: and this second Jury is called a Jury of Traverse: If the first Jury was a Jury of four of the Parish, the Jury of Traverse must be a Jury of six; that is, two of every Parish in the Sheading: If the first was a Jury of six, that is, a Sheading-Jury, then the Jury of Traverse must be a Jury of 12, of the Sheading: And if that Jury of 12, also, do not find for him as he expected, he may have a Jury of 12 of

the 24 Keyes of the Island, to passe upon his matter; and that
is a definitive end of the businesse. And as the Lord had the
Forfeiture of 3*l.* upon the first Jury of Traverse, he is likewise
to have the Forfeiteure of 3*l.* upon the second; and so of the
third also, if it fall so out, that none of the Juries of Traverse
find the first Jury in an errour; but these Fines are commonly
mittigated, sometimes to 5*s.* or 10*s.* sometimes to lesse, at
the discretion of the Debet-Court; whereof I shall speak
more hereafter.

Goal-Delivery.

After all these Sheading-Courts are done, which continue
as before is said, a Fortnight; then upon the Monday after, is
the Head-Court, or Court of Goal-Delivery, where the
Prisoners are arraigned and tryed by a Jury of the Countrey,
chosen most commonly but one of a Parish: The Fellon or
Delinquent having before been indicted by a Jury of six of
the Sheading wherein he lived, if the fact was done in the
same Sheading: And if he lived in one Sheading, and
committed the Fact in another, then the Jury of Indictment
must be three of the Sheading where he lived; and three of
the Sheading where the Fact or Crime was committed: This
Jury of Indictment is taken by the Coroner of the Sheading
(or by both Coroners, if it fall out, as in the last case
aforesaid), immediately after the apprehending of the
Delinquent. And the Coroner brings the Jury and the
Delinquent also, before the Controllour most commonly; or,
it may be, before the Governour, or one of the Deemsters, or
both; and they take notice how the Jury finds the businesse:
And if it be so, that they find him in fault by the Evidence
which they have received then or before, they leave him
indicted, which is entred upon Record by the Controllor:
And upon this Record, the Form of his Arraignment and

Tryall, at the Goal-delivery is drawn up; and the Jury, of 12 of the Countrey, passes upon the Delinquent; and one Jury of 12 serves for all the Prisoners at the Bar; for the Delinquents may all, or any of them, have their just Exceptions against those that shall be brought in to pass upon their lives: But, in conclusion, the whole 17 Parishes being there, a Jury will be had, which the prisoners must abide: Then this Jury of Life and Death, when they are ready with their Verdict, they come again before the Court; and the Deemster asks if the Bald-pate may sit or no, while they deliver their Verdict: if any of the prisoners at the Bar be by them found guilty, as that by the Law they are to dye, the Jury says, the Bald-pate may not sit: Then the Bishop and all his Clergy, (when time was,) who have been all the time before in Court, must depart the Court, while the Verdict is delivered, and Judgment given by the Deemster. If the matter of Fact, by the Delinquent, be for Felony, to the value of 6*d*. *ob*. or above, it is Felony to death: if for breaking a Fire-house, either the Wall, or the Door thereof; or if there be no door but a bundle of Gorse, or Ling, reared up in the door, to keep the wind out, or but two sticks put crosse in the door, it is Burglary, and Death to the Delinquent, though it be for Fellony under the value aforesaid, if the Fellony be done by a man, his Judgment is, to hang till he be dead; if by a Woman, by the Old Law, to be put in a Sack, and drowned in the water; but, of late the Women also have Judgment to be hang'd as the men. If the matter be for Witchcraft, the Delinquent shall be burned.

The Evidence against such a Delinquent, is taken by Spirituall Officers (it was in the time of Episcopacy so) and by them certified to the Temporal Court, by, and upon the Oaths of 12 Jurors, and of the Chapter-quests, and Side-men of the several Parishes; and after this, the Jury of Life and Death, at the Court of Goal-Delivery, passes upon the party, as upon other Fellons. If it be for the death of any one, committed by violence of hand, or poysoning, it is death to the party that did the Fact, without priviledge of Clergy, or benefit of Plea of Chance-medly; for which in other places, the prisoner might have his book; but here, there is no such matter, nor no remedy, but the Lords grace: And for all manner of Fellony, Murder, Witchcraft, or such like, where the prisoner is adjudged to die, the Lord hath the Forfeiture of the Lands, Tenements, Goods, and Chattels of such Delinquent: but if such a Delinquent had a wife, and was a year and a day married, before the time of the offence committed, then such wife shall not lose her Widow-right, neither of the Goods nor Lands, but shall have her part thereof cleer, paying her proportionable share of the Debts: And all such as have any debts owing to them by the Delinquent must come in to the Controller, or the Lords Atturney, and put in their Claims betwixt the time of the Indictment & the Tryall by the Jury of Life and Death, otherwise they lose their debts, as to the Lords part of the Delinquents estate: Out of these Goods and Personall Estate of the Delinquent so forfeited, as aforesaid, the Coroner of the Sheading, who is to do the execution himself, or procure it to be done, is to have all these quick Goods, as Horses, Mares, Bullocks, or Heiffers, of two years old, or under, and all such goods also, as by the Law should have fallen to the next Heir, as Coarbes, the Coroner is to have them.

Swine to the Lord: Goats to the Queen.

All Swine, of what age soever, are the Lords, and all Goats of what age soever, belong to the Queen of Man.

The Coroner also usually hath the broken sacks of Corn of the Fellons, which are not absolutely due to him, as it should seem by the words of the Statute: Now out of these

goods, which the Coroner is to have, as aforesaid, the
Deemster is to have 4*s*. and the Moor 4*s*. and the rest is his
own; a woman, as before is said, forfeits nothing for the Fact
of her husband; but the husband, if his wife commit Fellony,
and he knows of it, and conceals it, he stands as deep in the
Law, in all cases of Forfeiture, of body, of goods, and estate,
as she doth.

Bishop and Abbots demand a Prisoner.

Furthermore, it is to be remembred, that if the Tenant of
any Baron in the Island, as heretofore of the Bishop, Abbots,
and now the Tenants of Banchor, Sabale, &c. commit Fellony,
such a Fellon coming to the Bar of the Court of Goal-
delivery, with the rest of the Fellons, before the Governour
and Deemsters; the Steward of such Baron, whose Tenant
such Fellon is, may demand the prisoner from the Bar, and
he shall have him delivered, to be tryed at such his Lord
Barons Court; where, neverthelesse, the Lord of the Island's
Deemsters are to sit also as Judges, the Forfeiture of the Lands
holden of the Baron, are the Barons; the goods also of the
Delinquent, paying no Rent to the Lord of the Island, at the
time of the Fellony committed, nor hath not served a year
and a day upon the Lords Land, nor was not born upon the
Lords Land; in any of which cases, the Lord of the Island hath
the Forfeiture of the goods; and howsoever the sole disposure
of the body of the Delinquent, to do with him as he please.

What else, at the Goal-delivery.

Other businesse there is at the Court of Goal-delivery; as
chiefly, the great Inquests of every Sheading, which were
sworn at the Sheading-Courts, the half year before; come in
then, and present their annoyances of the Countrey and

State, in that half year before, which were given them in charge at the Sheading-Courts to inquire of: then the Recognizances of the Peace are called, and the bonds released, if no man can ought say against the party bound thither; If any complain, either new bonds are taken for the peace, till the next Court of Goal-delivery; or the same Recognizance stands, with a Note of Continuance, &c.

Clerk of the Courts nothing.

And this is a most remarkable token of the Lords: goodness and nobleness of the Lord of the Land, that the Clerk of the Court hath not a Farthing for the according of any Recognizance of the Peace, or at the releasing thereof, nor for the recording of the Indictment of any Delinquent, or the drawing up of the Order of Arraignment, nor the entering of any Action at the Common-Law, though there be an infinite number at every Court; nor for the recording of any Presentment, brought in by the great Inquests of the Sheadings, or Juries of slander; or any other businesse whatsoever, handled at the Sheading-Courts, or Courts of Goal-delivery,

Bishops Court.

There are some other Courts of Judicature also, which are after the same Rules of the Common-Law, as aforesaid; and which are kept immediately after the Lords Courts are ended. As the Bishops Court for his Temporalities; where also the Lords Deemsters are Judges, and his Controller the Register or Clerk of the Rolls; for the keeping of which Courts, the Deemsters have 2-0-0 per annum from the Bishop, and the Controller 2-0-0.

Abbey- Courts[67] *Courts of Bangor, Sabal, and St. Trinions.*

The Courts for the Abbey-Lands also are kept by the same Officers of the Lords; and so are the Courts for the Baronies of Bangor, Sabal, and St. Trinions, the Fees to the Deemsters, from the Abbot, are 26*s*. 8*d*. per annum, and the like to the Controller. The Fees for Bangor, Sabal, and St. Trinions, are 13*s*. 4*d*. to the Deemsters, and 13*s*. 4*d*. to the Controller.

The proceedings of these Courts, are after the same order, as those of the Lords Courts, viz. First, the Court-Leet; before which, the Deemster gives the Charge to the 12 men sworn upon the great Inquest: then follows the blood-quest; and last of all, the Conrt-Baron, for matters of right betwixt party and party; and this is the end of the Common-Law-Courts.

Court of Debet.

After all these, follows the Court of Debet, which is the Court for assessing of the Fines of all the Courts for the whole year, both Lords and Barons; and this Court is kept commonly upon the Wednesday, after the Head-Court day after Michaelmas: the Officers of this Court of Assessment, or asseasing of the Fines, are the Governour, the two Deemsters,[68] the Controller, Receiver, Water-Bailiff, and the Lords Atturney,: but the Barons, as the Bishop, the Abbot, and the rest, have no voyces nor hand in the assessment of the Fines; no, not of the Fines of their own Courts: yet shall they have the Fines and Perquisites of their own Courts, after they are assessed by the Lords Officers, as aforesaid, viz. of all such of their Tenants, as properly and solely are their own Tenants, and pay no rent to the Lord of the Island, nor were not born, nor had served a year and a day, as Apprentices, upon the Lords Lands; for in all such cases, the Lord of the

Island hath the Fines and Amerciaments, be the Tenants of what Barony soever.

The Fines out in Charge.

After the end of all these Common-Law-Courts, the Controller collects and estreats out the Fines, of every Court, both Lords and Barons, and gives them out in charge to the Moors, which they are to collect, and pay them in to the Receiver, with the Land-rent of the several Parishes, and such Fines as belong solely to the Barons, he gives them out to the Serjeants or Bayliffs of the Barons, to be collected for the use of the Baron to whom they belong.

Exchequer Court.

There is another Court, which the Governour, and the Lords Officers aforesaid, do keep as often as occasion requires; sometime in one place, sometime in another Circuit of the Countrey, as businesse falls out; and that is called an Exchequer Court: At these Courts, such Juries of Tryals betwixt party and party, as could not give in their Verdicts' at the Sheading-Courts, bring them in then: And Juries also of slander, Juries of Presentment of Misdemeanours, and Juries of Indictment, of Felony, (if any such be) bring in their Verdicts at these Courts: so that whatsoever businesses could not be well determined at Term-times, or Sheading-courts, they are deliberately heard and determined at some of these Exchequer-courts, winch is a mighty great ease and conveniency to the Subject, and not much troublesome to the Officers.

Chancery Court.

There is also a Court of Chancery (which hath not been

long erected) kept by the Governour, whereof he sits sole Judge, as Chancellour, representing the Lords person; which Court he may keep every week once, as occasion shall require, (and especially in cases of strangers, who desire speedy Tryals of their businesse) the Plaintiff may come to the Controller, and enter his complaint for 3*d*. and thereof take a Copy, and shew it to the Governour; he gives him a Token, (which is some mark he useth to make) upon a stone of blew Slate, which are plentiful, or to be had every where in the Island: The Plaintiff delivers this to the Coroner of the place where the Defendant lives (if he be an Islander) and if the Defendant be a stranger, and but a sojourner in some part of the Island, then he delivers the Token to the Water-Bayliff; and to which soever of them he gives this Token, he gives him also but 2*d*. And that Coroner, or the Water-Bayliff, or his Deputies, (some of the Customers) who the party can be shewed unto by the Complainant, shall summon this Defendant three days before the day the Governour hath assigned the Plaintiff to follow his Action or Complaint; if the Defendant appear not at that Court, the Plaintiff pays a groat to the Controller, and craveth an Attachment, to charge him for the next Court, and the Governour delivers out another Token, and appoints the day he shall appear: And if he appear not, then a second Attachment is awarded, and he pays 12*d*. more. And if he stand out that Processe, a Souldier goes out to bring him in at the next Court after, and he must have a shilling also for that service, where then he must of force appear (if he be an Islander) upon pain of Forfeiture of body and goods; and if he be a stranger, the Water-Bayliff will secure himself at the first Summons; either the Defendant shall put in bayl, to answer and save him and the Court harmlesse, or else he will crave authority from the Governour, to commit his body to prison.

Then when the Defendent is brought to his appearance,

the matter goes to a Hearing: the Governour having called to him if he please, one or both of the Deemsters for their advices in matter of Law, or all or any of the Lords Council, as he shall think fit, he makes his Decree, as he shall find cause in Equity; from which Decree or Order, the Defendant, if the Decree be against him, may appeal to the Lord of the Island, and have a certain time limited by the Court, for the bringing in of his Lordships Order, putting in Surety, to answer the Demands, as the Lord shall direct, or as the Court shall order: In the meantime, Execution which should have been given out by the Governour upon the Decree, shall stay till the time limited be out: And if no Order come to the contrary, it is to proceed by vertue of the Governours Token to the Coroner, for the taking of a Pawn, if it be for a debt; or for delivery of possession, if it be for Land; against which, if the Defendant stand out, the Coroner presents, and a Souldier goes out to assist the Coroner in executing of the fermer Execution, and to bring the party disobeying to prison, there to remain, till he shall submit to the Order.

And if there be an Action depending at the Common-Law betwixt party and party, the Defendant may at any time before Issue joyned, that is, before he have appeared, and put his businesse to the tryall of a Jury, procure the Governours Token to stay the proceedings at the Common-Law, and then the cause may be proceeded in by the Chancery, and the party grieved have relief, as the Court shall find cause in Equity; otherwise, the Court will dismiss the Cause back to the Common-Law, with Costs, for wrongfull vexation; and all the charges the Complainant lays out in this Court of Chancery, is but 3s. 1d. if the Defendant stand out to the utmost; and 3d. for the Copy of the said Entry of his Complaint, be the cause of never so great value, the 3s. 4d. the Court will award for the Plaintiff, if he recover, and other charges besides, as shall be thought fit. And of this 3s. 4d. the

Controller accompts for 1*s*. 6*d*. thereof to the Lord: The Coroner hath 6*d*. for the three Summons of the Defendant; and the Souldier 12*d*. for bringing him in at the last.

Execution in Chancery and Common-Law.

The manner of this execution, by taking of the Defendants pawn, both upon the Governours Token, upon Cases in the Chancery, and of the Deemsters, in Cases at the Common-Law, is this; The Coroner goes (with a copy of the Decree in Chancery, or of the Verdict of the Jury at the Common-Law) to the Defendants house, and demands a pawn, which he may deny, if he please; and then the Officer makes his presentment of the disobedience, which is recorded by the Controller. Then the Plaintiff procures a copy of that Presentment, and shews it to the Governour; who hereupon delivers him his Token to the Constable of the Castle, for a Souldier to go with, and assist the Officer, which was so before disobeyed: then the Coroner, by the authority and aid of the Souldier, takes the Pawn by force, *viz.* so much goods of the Defendant, as is double the value of the debt recovered; which Pawn so taken is to be put in some Neighbours house or keeping; and the same is called by the Officer, the three Sundays after; and if the party that owes the goods, nor none for him, will release the goods, by the payment of the debt: then the Officer causeth the pawn to be brought to the Market-crosse, or to the Parish-church, and there to be praised by four men; and sold immediately, if any man will buy it: if no man will buy it, the four men are to take it by Praisment; the Coroner or Officer to receive the money, and pay the debt to the Plaintiff, and restore the rest to the Defendant: If it be a businesse at the Common-Law, the Moor of the Parish upon the Deemsters token may execute the recovery as well as the Coroner in the former;

and neither of them shall have above 2*d*. for the doing of the duty; and the Souldier (if it come to the extremity aforesaid) 1*s*. There is a Fee of 2*d*. upon every recovery at the Common-Law due to the Deemster for his Token, and these are all the fees that are due, and are to be taken out of the Defendants pawn, besides the debt to the party; But it is to be remembred, that the Defendant by the Law forfeits 6*s*. 8*d*. for denying his pawn to the Coroner, or more, at the first demanding of it, which Fine is most commonly mitigated to 1*s*. And if he withstand or disobey the Souldier, he forfeits body and goods by the Law, and is to be brought to prison by the Souldier, who may call unto him (if need be) for his Ayd, the Coroner of the Sheading to raise the Country or Sheading to assist him. Lastly, it is a very considerable good Order they have in this Island, for the easie end in determing of ordinary businesse betwixt party and party: A man that hath cause of complaint against another for a debt or other matter, may procure the Governours Token or the Deemsters, to bring his adverse party before either of them; And if the Defendant do confesse the debt or matter, or that it appear by the evidence of two Witnesses upon their Oaths, that such a debt or thing is due, either of the said Officers may give their Token for execution to the Coroner or Lockman; and this is as good and Lawfull as if the matter had received Triall by verdict of a Jury, or Decree in the Chancery, so that either of these two Officers are in effect Courts of Record in themselves; though they be but walking or riding in the High way, (if cases of such like condition come before them) and all their Acts and proceedings in this kind as effectuall as if they had been done in Court, which is a great ease to the Subject.

Lockman is an under-Sheriffe.

The prospect of Castell Rushen in the Isle of Man on y.e South side

The Prospect of Peel Castell in y.e Isle of Man on y.e West side

A. Ireland
B. Wales

The Prospect of Douglas in y.e Isle of Man on the East side

Who Justices of the Peace in all places.

The Deemsters are in all places in the Island, where they come, Justices of the Peace; As if they see or be informed of any force or battery to be committed by any manner of person, they may take Recognisance for the Peace in the Lords name, and certifie them into the Controllers or Clerk of the Rolls Office; or if that be denyed, or that sufficient Bayl or Sureties for the Peace be not tendered unto them, they may commit the Delinquent to the Coroner of the Sheading, where they then are at that instant, and he is to bring the parly to the next Gaol; or if he be near unto any of the Garrison places of Castle-Rushen, Castle-Peel,[69] or Douglas Fort, he or they may send such Delinquent to the Constable thereof to be committed till the Governour have opportunity, or give further or other order in the businesse: The Controller, Receiver, Water-Bayliff may do the like, and the Lords Atturney for preservation of the Peace, and the Coroner who is the Sheriffe, or the Lockman his under-Sheriffe, may take Recognizances of the Peace, and return them aforesaid into the Office, as well as any of the other Officers; but he may not commit the party, but may raise the Country to assist him to bring him before the Governour or some Officer that may commit him.

What further power the Deemsters have.

The Deemster may do likewise many other lawfull Acts by their places; as namely, They put out Juries ex Officio, for furnishing the Lords Tenants with servants every man according to his holding: the sons or servants of the Tenants of lesser rents are to serve the Tenants of greater rents in cases of extremity, if vagrant servants cannot be had; and some Officers, as the Deemsters, the Moors and Coroners are to have their choice of servants. The Parsons also of Parishes, and Vicars of thirds of Tithes of such Parish are to have the like; which is called their Bridge and Staffe. The Deemsters for a debt for Corn upon the Plaintiffs Oath gives his Token for Execution without hearing of the matter: Also if one Beast kill another, he puts out a Jury presently to try the matter; and as he finds by the Verdict of that Jury, he gives his Execution, for the delivery of the living beast for the dead or damages, as he shall find cause; but many times such matters he refers to the Common-Law.

The Receivers Duty.

The Receiver, by his place, is the chief Officer for the collecting of the Lords Rents, he may commit the Moors or Bayliffs for their neglects in not taking them up in due time from the Tenants; And when the Moors are so committed, his Token to the Constable commands a Souldier to fetch in the Tenants; but the Moores before this ought to take the pawns of the Tenants, and cause them to be praised and sold for payment of the rent.

The Controuller's Duty.

The Controuller is by his place to call the Receiver to Accompt once every quarter, and may sit by and take notice at all times when the Receiver takes money from the Moors, and take notice of what is paid: He is also to have knowledge, and give check or allowance of all payments and disbursements by the Receiver, and to keep his book thereof, and at the end of the year to set the Debet, and perfect the Accompts betwixt the Receiver and the Moors. He is also to give out the Water-Bayliffe his charge soon after Midsummer, having upon the Midsummer-day before received from the

Governour his Book of Licences and Entries for Outgates
and Ingates of Commodities: He is also by his place Clerk of
the Market, and is to see to the Weights and Measures of all
sorts, and the Assize of Bread and Ale, that it be duly kept:
And he is also head-searcher in all the Ports, that by his
Deputies or under-searchers the Lord may not be abused or
wronged in his Customs.

The Water-Bayliff's Duty.

The Water-Bayliff is by his place, by himself and his
under-Officers, the Customers of the Ports of Ramsey,
Duglas, Derby-haven, and Peel-town, to take up and
faithfully to collect all the Customs for Ingates and Outgates
of Goods: Also it is his place as he is Admirall, to order all
the businesse for the Herring-Fishery, to see that Strangers
and all others have no wrong done them during that Season,
and to Judge of and determine by way of Jury, which is called
an Admirall-Quest, of all matters betwixt party and party in
matters of Seafaring businesse: He is also to give out Cockets
of Goods that shall be exported: And to take notice and
cognisance of Cockets from other parts, of such goods as
shall be imported; and thereof to make certificate at the suit
or request of the Merchant. All Wrecks of Sea he is likewise
to take care of; that they be disposed of for the Lord's profit,
and to make return of his proceedings therein to the
Controuler, that they may be recorded, and the venditions
thereof made, put out in charge: In this last particular the
Lord's Atturney's care is likewise required, and the businesse
may be done by either of them, as it lyes in their quarters or
way where they shall come.

The Lord's Atturney's Duty.

The Lord's Atturney is to plead and stand for the Lord's profit in all cases, and in the cases of Widowes and Infants, who have Causes in Court: He ought to be in all Courts both Spirituall and temporall, to take notice of the Fines and Forfeitures to the Lord. He is to take care and enquire of all Wayffs and Strays, Felons goods, Deodands, Wrecks of Sea, and such like, which are due to the Lord by his prerogative: And the Lords Receiver and He, are to sell and dispose of them to the Lord's best profit, and present the values from time to time to the Controuler, that he may put the moneys due for them out in the next charge.

In all these or any other matters wherein every or any of the said Officers have to deal, the Lieutenant or Governour is to call them to Accompt as he shall see cause upon complaint, or otherwise at his own discretion; and if any of them shall have done or proceeded otherwise then according to Law, or have been neglective in their places, he is to certifie their offence to his Lordship; And for the present may commit the body of such Officer or Officers, in case he conceive danger of his or their further misdemeanour, or departure out of the Country without his consent. And this is to the end that such Officer may be forth-coming to make good and answer according to his Lordships Order or Command, which shall be returned upon the Certificate made as aforesaid by the Governour.

To conclude this Chapter; This Island, ever since the reducing of it by Sir William Mountacute, hath been reputed, and is a member of England; and held of the Crown thereof sometime by one Tenure, and sometime by another; and now at this day the Lord thereof holdeth it of the Common-Wealth of England by Fealty onely; notwithstanding it hath Lawes and Customes peculiar to itself, which are most suitable to its Poverty and distance from England.[70]

CHAPTER V.

CONCERNING THE TRADE OF THE ISLE.

———————

THE Trade of this Island in regard it produceth not any Commodities of value, neither is improved by way of Manufacture; nor hath Merchants nor Shipping belonging to it, hardly deserveth a Chapter by itself.[71]

The Commodities of the Country.

The Trade for Exportation consisteth in Hides, the skins of sheep and Goats, a small quantity of Herrings, and Corn when the Island is first assured there is enough to serve itself. The forrain Commodities they want are Wood, Iron, Salt, Pitch and Tarre; without these they cannot live: as for Wines, Spices, &c. these poor people make no reckoning of; being contented with such homely accomodations for dyet and clothing as their own Country affordeth. It is traded with 4 Market-Towns, Castle-Town, Douglas, Peel-Town and Ramsey. A Manufacture of their Wools might here be profitably erected; for we see Jersey, that hath no Wooll within itself, considerable; yet it maintaineth a great Trade with the Woolls there wrought, and brought from other Countries.

Worth the observing for their Commerce with strangers, from Mr. Tynsly the Atturney Generall.

Further, for matter of profit to the Islanders for Trade and Commerce with other Nations, this is the manner There are four Merchants which are ever chosen by the Country; which choice is usually made at the Tyn-wald Court, and sworn by the Deemsters to deal truly, and most for the Countries profit; these for the present are Mr. John Stanley, and Mr. Philip Moor for the South side; and Mr.

Thomas Crelling, and Mr. David Christian for the North side: These when any Ship of Salt, Wines, Pitch, Iron, or other Commodities good for the use of the Country, comes into the Island, the Governour having first consulted with the Merchant-Stranger about the rates and prices of the Commodities, he sends then for these four Merchants of the Country to appear before him and the Merchant-Stranger; and drives a bargain if he can, betwixt them; if he cannot agree with them, he commands the 4 Merchants to spend another day with the Merchant-stranger, to deal with him if they can. And whatsoever bargain is made by the said 4 Merchants, the Country is to stand to it, and take the Commodities of the Merchant-stranger and pay for them by and according to the rates agreed upon; which most commonly is, that the Country are to bring in their Commodities of Wooll, Hides, Tallow, and such like, and for the same have their equall proportions of the Commodities of Salt, Wine, Iron, Pitch, &c. so brought in and compounded for, as aforesaid. And if the Commodities brought in by the Country will not extend to the value of the Strangers Commodities, then the 4 Merchants are to assesse the rest of the Commodities upon the Country every one his equall proportion; for which they are to pay ready moneys as the four Merchants had agreed for them. So by this means the Merchant-stranger is much encouraged to bring in necessary things for the Island, and the people have by the faithfulnesse of their 4 Merchants, the full benefit of the commodity brought in; which otherwise some private man of the Country might, and would have taken for his own profit: And this is an especiall benefit for the enriching of the people, and for the generall good.

CHAPTER VI.

OF THE STRENGTH OF THE ISLAND.

———————

THIS Island is secured mightily by nature; not onely in that it is an Island; but also for that it is situated in a very boysterous Sea, encompassed on all sides with high Cliffs of stone, or precipices of Sand, saving on the North part about the Point of Ayre; where the shoar is low and beachie, so that Ships in fair weather may ride near the Land, in all other parts of the Coast, by reason of the rocks that lye far into the Sea; there is no coming near the shoar with safety, nor entring their Roads or Harbour without a Pilot; nor Anchoring in their Roads unlesse the same be a Lee-shore.

The Bodies of the Inhabitants are made use of for its defence; for every Parish hath a Captain, under whom are listed, disciplined and arm'd, such as are meet for the War, of whom they have about 1500 ready upon occasion; and in case of necessity, I believe they might arm 5 or 6000 Men.

It is fortified with a Castle at Rushen, the strongest pile of stone that I have seen; pleasantly situated, rather then usefully, in a flat Country, a Rivelet running beneath it; but this Castle standeth at such a distance from the shallow and rocky Harbour of Rushen, that it is of no consequence to hinder the landing of an enemy there; which considered, the late E. of Derby raised a Fort hard by at Lanquet-Point,[72] for the securing of that Harbour and Rainsway. Tradition saith, this Castle of Rushen[73] was built by the Norwegians; this I read of it. That Magnus the last K. of Man of that Race dyed there in the year 1265. and before that I find no mention of it. Also with Peel-Castle situated in St. Patrick's Isle, impregnable towards the Sea; yet, though seated in an

Island, the Sea forsakes it, at low water, and from a Hill near it, they may be in such sort annoyed, that they cannot without much danger stir abroad in the Castle-Yard.

Duglas Fort.

There is a Block-House at Duglas,[74] a round Fabrick of stone, which may serve to secure the Road and Harbour sufficiently from Pickroons; which is as much as the condition of the place or Isle requireth.

At Ramsey there are also a few Guns mounted, sufficient also for that purpose.

It were to be wished, that some Fortification were made about the Point of Ayre; which the E. of Derby in the time of the late Troubles did perform; but now neglected and ruin'd: when also he made a Fort in the middest of the Island,[75] generally held to be of no consequence, he alledging it to be for the better corresponding with the other places of strength in times of service; and probably he might have in his eye the awing of the Natives, which in the condition he then stood in, he might have some cause to mistrust: But to conclude, when all is said that can be spoken upon this Head; the Poverty of this Island is its greatest Security.

FINIS.

NOTES BY THE EDITOR.

———————

Note 1.—"Thomas, Lord Fairfax." (Epistle Dedicatory)

Thomas, Lord Fairfax, the eldest son of Ferdinando, Lord Fairfax, was born at Denton, in 1601. He was educated at St. John's College Cambridge, and subsequently served as a volunteer in Holland, under Horatio, Lord Vere, of Tilbury, in Essex, whose daughter Anne, he at a later period married. He was present at the taking of Bois le Duc. On returning to England, he retired into private life. The Civil War recalled him to military enterprise on the Parliamentary side, and he was made General of the Horse, under his father. In this capacity he met with varying fortune in the North of England, which the battle of Marston Moor, in 1644, ultimately determined in his favor. In all instances his valour, enterprise, and zeal, were so conspicuous, that on the resignation of the Earl of Essex, in 1645, he was appointed to succeed him as General of the Army, which had been remodelled and recruited. His commission did not run like that of Essex, in the name of the King and Parliament; but in that of the Parliament alone: and the article concerning the King's safety was omitted. A medal of Sir Thomas Fairfax bears on the obverse his bust regarding the left, with the encircling legend "Gener: Tho: Fairfax: Miles: Milit: Parli: Dux." The battle of Naseby, in 1645, proved him in every way worthy of the trust reposed in him. Whilst, however, the whole military authority was in appearance devolved on Lord Fairfax, it was, through the machinations of the Independents, really exercised by Cromwell. Fairfax was in truth too good and honest a man for the party to which he was attached. His moderation in the hour of triumph was remarkable; and on the surrender of Oxford, he was particularly careful to preserve the Bodleian Library and other places, from pillage; and it has been said that through his influence, the University suffered less from the Parliamentary troops, than it had done from those of the Royalists.

Subsequently he caused the Royalists to raise the siege of Taunton, and then beat them from Lamport, took successively Bridgewater and Sherborne, and laid siege to Bristol, which surrendered to him September the 10th, 1645. This was the ruin of the King's cause, for it led to his retirement to Oxford for the winter, and in the beginning of the next year, on Lord Fairfiix approaching with a powerful army, to his flight to the Scottish forces at Newark. The capture of Raglan Castle, in 1646, made Fairfax master of the situation. The venality of the Scotch in their surrender of the King to the Parliament, for the sum of £400,000, Jan. 30th, 1647, is well known.

The greatest stain on the Character of this great man, was the execution of Sir Charles Lucas and Sir George Lisle, on the surrender of Colchester, after an eleven weeks siege, in 1648; and his treacherous explanation of the terms granted to Lord Capel, which brought that nobleman to the block.

Fairfax behaved with the greatest respect towards his Sovereign in his humiliation; and even seemed desirous of restoring him to the throne. His partiality was in fact so far suspected, that though nominated for one of the Judges on the King's pretended trial (in which office, however, he refused to serve), on the day of Charles's execution, it was deemed necessary to engage Fairfax in prayer and conference, at Major Harrison's, till the fatal blow had been struck, lest he should interfere to prevent the carrying out the sentence of death.

It is said that he was much influenced in his conduct towards the King by his wife, whose feelings were so strong, that when the indictment against Charles was read, and the Clerk came to the words "all the good people of England," she exclaimed aloud in court, "no, not the hundredth part of them." It was also thought necessary to appease the resentment of Fairfax, consequent on the execution of Charles, by appointing him Generalissimo of the forces employed in England and Ireland; and under this commission he suppressed the Levellers, who were becoming formidable in Oxfordshire.

In 1650, the Scotch declared for Charles the Second; and when it was determined to make war against them, Fairfax was looked to for its conduct, but he yielded to his wife's interposition, and chose rather to throw up his appointment and retire into private life, with a pension of £5,000 per annum. He had succeeded his father, in March, 1648, in his titles; and thus united the hereditary dignity of the Peerage with the honor which he had acquired by his bravery. After the political murder of James, the Seventh Earl of Derby, who was beheaded at Bolton, on the 15th of October, 1651, the Parliament granted to Lord Fairfax, in addition to his other estates, the Seignory of the Isle of Man, "in public gratitude for his high deserts, and not as the issue of his own desires."

His noble feeling and devotion to literature and religion were here also conspicuous; for he set apart the proceeds of the sequestered Bishopric, to the increase of the incomes of the inferior Clergy, and the establishment of Grammar Schools, in the four towns of the Isle of Man—Castletown, Douglas, Peel, and Ramsey.

At the eve of the Restoration, he determined to make peace with the exiled King. He induced Lambeth's Irish troops to join Monk's army, and was at the head of the Commissioners appointed to wait upon Charles the Second, at the Hague, to invite him to return to England, and assume the crown. He was well received; and having performed the commission entrusted to him, retired into the country, where he composed his "Memorials of the War"; and died on the 12th November, 1671, in the seventieth year of his age. He held the Lordship of the Isle of Man eight years.

He had, by his wife Anne, one only daughter, born in 1686, and married to George Villiers, Second Duke of Buckingham, and who died in 1704. He was succeeded by his cousin Henry (grandson of the First Lord Fairfax), as Fourth Baron. Henry died in 1693, aged 86, without issue. Then his estates devolved to his sister's son, Philip Martin (who took the name of Fairfax), a Lieutenant-General in the army. Bryan, Eighth Baron in direct descent, heir of the last Lord, and whose father had acquired property in Virginia, came to England from America, in 1793, and laid claim to the Peerage, which was allowed by the House of Lords, in 1800; and in 1808, the House of Commons voted him £20,000 in compensation for his losses in Virginia. He, however, returned to America, and married a Miss Elizabeth Cary, by whom he had several children. It is said that he entered Holy Orders, and became a D.D., in the United States.

Lord Fairfax was, to judge from his portraits, of a manly aspect, but of a gloomy disposition. In his manners he was gentle and courteous; liberal in his principles, but sincere, open, and disinterested; and though possessed of only moderate talents, he was, from what we have seen in his conduct both at Oxford and in connection with the Isle of Man, a lover of literature, and a great patron of learning. The Manx were peculiarly fortunate in obtaining from amongst the Parliamentarians such a successor in the Lordship of the Isle to that great and good man, the unfortunate James, the Seventh Earl of Derby. The portrait of Lord Fairfax, given in this edition, is not in the original work of Chaloner.

Note 2.—"James Chaloner." (Epistle Dedicatory)

James Chaloner (our author), was fourth son of Thomas
Chaloner, of Guisborough, in Yorkshire (Knighted in 1591,
and died 1615), by his first wife Elizabeth, daughter of
William Fleetwood, Esq., Recorder of London. 'He was born
in London in 1603, and at the age of 13 years, he became a
Commoner of Brazenose College, in Oxford. According to
Wood (*Athenoe Oxonienses*, vol. ii., p. 161), he continued
there three or four years, and then went either to travel or to
the Inns of Court. On the breaking out of the Civil War, he
joined the fortunes of the Parliamentary party, and was
chosen as a Recruiter to sit for Aldborough, in Yorkshire, in
the Long Parliament. He took the Solemn League and
Covenant, and sided with the Independents. Having married
Ursula Fairfax, daughter of Sir William Fairfax, of Steeton,
in Yorkshire, he was thus brought into close connection with
Thomas, Lord Fairfax, and with him was chosen one of the
Judges of King Charles the First; having, in the previous year,
1647, been appointed Secretary to the Committee for the
reformation of the University of Oxford. The Isle of Man
having been granted by Parliament to Lord Fairfax, Chaloner
was named by him, August 17th, 1652, a Commissioner
(along with Robert Dinely, Esq., and Joshua Witton, Minister
of the Gospel,) for administering his Lordship's affairs in the
Island. The present treatise is the result of his labours on that
occasion; and his diligence appears to have been so fully
appreciated by Fairfax, that he was appointed to the
Governorship of the Island, in 1658, and continued in that
office till 1660. He does not appear to have taken as much
interest in the Restoration as his patron. On being sent for to
London, apprehending the consequences of the leading part
he had taken in the sentence on Charles the First, he
anticipated judgement by taking poison. Wood says, that in
March or April, 1660, messengers were sent from the

Superior Power to take James Chaloner into custody, and to secure his castle for the use of His Majesty; "but he having received timely notice of their coming, dispatched away himself by poison, taken, as 'tis said, in a posset made by his concubine, whom he then for several years had kept; leaving behind him a son named Edmund, of about 19 years of age, begotten on the body of his lawful wife."

He, at any rate, died in 1660, in his 58th year; and besides the son Edmund, born in 1635, left three daughters.

Of his literary abilities, and his zeal in antiquarian pursuits, we have both the testimony of his contemporaries, and evidence in the present work. He was esteemed, says Wood, as an ingenious and singular lover of antiquities. He made divers collections of arms, genealogies, seals, and monuments, from ancient evidences, of which he left records in various papers and books, which were afterwards perused by the learned Dr. Robert Sanderson, an eminent antiquary. He also made collections of arms, monuments, &c., in Staffordshire, Shropshire, and Cheshire; which came into the hands of John, son of Augustine Vernon, Windsor Herald, and were by him entitled *Chaloner's Collections for Staffordshire, Salop, and Chester*, and marked J.C. In the present work, Chaloner tells us that he caused several of the tumuli, with which the Isle of Man abounds, to be opened; and he has given us his views respecting their age and the people to whom they may be assigned. His devotion to heraldry and genealogical investigations, are seen in the documents which he has furnished as to Lord Beaumont, and the plate he has given us of the coats of arms of various branches of the Beaumont family. Very little of party bias can be observed in his writings. Not a word is written against the Earl of Derby, or the Governors appointed by him; and the candour of his statements respecting the condition of the Manx Church; the piety, zeal, and talents of the Bishops

Phillips and Parr, and the inferior Clergy, is very remarkable. It is nevertheless said in Gough's *History of the people called Quakers*, (Dublin, 1789,) that "He had been a violent persecutor; and was heard to say a little before his death, that he would quickly rid the Island of Quakers."

Note 3.—"The Inhabitants call it Manning."

Or rather "Ellan Vannin." "Ellan" signifying Island; and "Vannin" constructed from "Mannin," by the softening of the first mutable consonant, according to the Grammar of the Manx language—See vol. ii., *Manx Society*, pp. 6, 11, 26. A favorite expression of the natives is, "Eln Vannin veg veen"; *i.e.*, "Dear little Isle of Man," literally "Isle of Man, little dear."

For the various names given to the Isle of Man, see vol. i. of *Manx Society*, note 23, p. 10.

Note 4.—"About Thirty Miles."

The centre of the Island is in latitude 54 deg. 15 min. north, and longitude 4 deg. 30 min. west. Its length in a direction N.E. by N., and S.W. by S., from the Point of Ayre to the Sound of the Calf, is 33¼ miles. The greatest breadth, at right-angles to this direction, is from Bank's Howe, near Douglas, to Ballanayre, north of Peel, 12¼ miles.

Note 5.—"Then Rainsway."

Rainsway, *Ronaldsway*, or Derbyhaven, is in the south-east of the Island. In early times it had the names Rognvald's-Vagr (Reginald's Bay), Rognalwath, Rannesway, and Ramsway; and it was regarded as the most important harbour in the island, on account of its proximity to Castletown. It was the scene of some of the most celebrated and stirring events in Manx History. Here, in 1250, John Dugalson, who had declared himself King of the Isles, was defeated in an engagement with the Manx. Here, too, the

Manx themselves were defeated by the Scotch, under John Comyn and Alexander Stewart, in 1270; and again, in 1316, by a band of Irish freebooters, under Richard Mandeville. In this bay, James, Seventh Earl of Derby (the "Great Stanlagh"), almost miraculously escaped assassination in 1650; a piece of ordonance, loaded with shot, being fired at him as he was returning in a boat from a Parliamentary ship which he had visited; on which occasion, Colonel Snaid, Colonel Richard Weston, and Philip Lucas, master of the boat, were shot dead on either side of him. See Registers of Parishes of Malew and of Marown, under date 1650.

Note 6.—"A Lee Shore."

Chaloner appears to use the phrase "Lee Shore," in a wrong sense, both in this passage and elsewhere, when he speaks of ships not anchoring in the roads, unless the same be a *Lee shore*. In each of these cases he evidently means that the shore is "to windward."

Note 7.—"Or the English Coast."

Great improvements have recently been made in the Harbours of the Isle of Man, and more important ones are in progress. The attention of Government was earnestly evoked to the great importance of establishing Harbours of Refuge here, for the northern area of the Irish Sea, by the late Sir William Hilary, as far back as 1830.

Note 8.—"Are Mountains."

The total surface of the Isle of Man is about 130,000 acres, of which 29,393 acres are mountainous. The sum total of cultivated lands paying tithes, is 80,458 acres; the commons, now in course of being enclosed, 30,788 acres. The Ayre of Bride and the Ayre of Andreas (fen lands), 2,395 acres; and the waste lands, rocks, and islets, about 10,000 acres.

Note 9.—"Maroun and Cubgreve."

It is not easy to determine what mountains are here referred to by Chaloner. There are no mountains of importance within the boundaries of Marown Parish; the high ground of Archollogan is hardly more than 700 feet above the level of the sea; and Mount Murray and Lord's Seat, just out of Marown Parish, are not much higher. Possibly by Cubgreve, the Mountain Greebah (the top of which is 1,591 feet above the sea level), is intended.

Note 10.—"Snawfell."

Snawfell (Snaefell or Snoefell, according to the orthography of Professor Munch, *snow mountain*), in the north of the Island, has a height of 2,024 feet above the level of the sea.

Note 11.—"Lawton Sheep."

For an account of the Lawton sheep, or rather Loaghtyn or Lugh-dhoan, i.e. *mouse-brown* sheep (*lugh* a "mouse," *dhoan* "brown"), See vol. i. *Manx Society*, note 31, p. 13.

Note 12.—"Herrings only."

The vast improvement, which has lately taken place in the agriculture and fisheries of the Isle of Man, will be seen on reference to note 68, infra.

Either Chaloner must have been misinformed as to the time of the migration of the herring and its appearance on the shores of the Isle of Man; or a change has taken place in the habits of the fish, which would prove interesting to Naturalists, could it be substantiated.

In the year 1827, a Committee of the House of Keys (the Manx Parliament) inquired into, and reported on the subject of the herring fishery, to the following effect:—

"It would appear that, contrary to the general received

opinion, a shoal or shoals of herrings enter St. George's Channel from the south, in the month of May, when the fishery commences near Arklow, on the Coast of Ireland, and that the progress of the fish to the northward is slow, Arklow, Ardglass, and the Isle of Man, being the successive fishing grounds frequented by the Cornish boats; that the fish seldom reaches the Isle of Man before the middle of June, or later; that two coral-banks, situated to the east and west of the island, and chiefly the former, would seem to be the ultimate annual destination of this shoal or shoals, these spots being uniformly frequented by them, for the purpose of therein depositing their spawn; that after the completion of this process, in the months of October and November, the shoals again return southward with greater expedition than they had advanced, and furnish a second, or winter fishing at Arklow, in November. In the summer fishery, the herrings are always caught with their heads to the north, *i.e.* on the south side of the net; and in the winter, they mesh with their heads to the south, *i.e.* on the north side of the net."

Note 13.—"Called Puffines."

Sacheverell, in his short survey of the Isle of Man (see vol. i. *Manx Society*, p. 13), has repeated this story of the puffin. He also states that William, Ninth Earl of Derby, stocked the Calf of Man with fallow-deer.—See also vol. i. *Manx Society*, note 33, p. 13.

Note 14.—"Oaks Digged up often from under Ground."

Sacheverell refers to the same fact.—See vol. i. *Manx Society*, p. 14. The drainage of the Great Curragh, in the north of the Isle of Man, which was anciently occupied by several lakes, commenced about the close of the 16th century. At a depth of from 18 to 20 feet in this Curragh, under the peat, were discovered the remains of trees, chiefly oak and fir, with their roots still firm in the ground, but their heads broken off, and lying towards the N.E. Bishop Wilson, in his *History of the Isle of Man*, p. 341, says:—"Some large trees of oak and fir have been found, some two feet and a half in diameter; they do not lie promiscuously, but where there is plenty of one sort, there are generally few or none of the other." These trees were probably contemporaneous with those forests which we find now submerged around the shores of the Isle of Man (more particularly at Strandhall, in Poolvash Bay), and which grew upon that drift-gravel terrace which once connected the Isle of Man with the surrounding coasts of Great Britain and Ireland. The basins containing the shell-marl, in which are found the remains of the Cervus Megaceros, lie underneath the turf beds and trees, in the gravel itself. They point to the period when the drift gravel was a wide treeless plain, roamed over by the herds of deer whose remains we now find in the marl, lying at the bottom of them.—See plate viii. of my *Isle of Man: Its History Physical, Ecclesiastical, Civil, and Legendary*.—Edit.

Note 15.—"Of which Stone, Castle Rushen was built."

Castle Rushen is *not* built of limestone from the Balladoole quarries, which is of a later age; but from the limestone of the same age as that on which the castle itself stands, either having been raised on the shore close by, or brought from the neighbourhood of the Stack of Scarlet. It is not improbable that under the name of quarries at Balladoole, our author refers to the quarries of black Posidonia-Schist, generally known as "Poolvash black marble," which are situated on the shore of Poolvash Bay, near Balladoole. It was from these quarries that the stone was procured which was presented by Bishop Thomas Wilson, for the steps of St. Paul's Cathedral, London, and also for the Parish Church of St. Peter's, in Lord Street, Liverpool, when built.—(See the *Chetham Society's Works*.) Many hundred tons per annum of the limestone of Ballahot and Port St. Mary, are now burnt into lime. Nearly 2,000 tons of the same kind of limestone are raised at Scarlet; about 100 tons of black marble from Poolvash; and the same quantity of Clay-Schist at Spanish Head; to which we have to add granite from Foxdale, and flagstones from S. Barrule.

Note 16.—"Captain Edward Christian."

Captain Edward Christian is one of the characters described in no very complimentary terms in Sir Walter Scott's *Peveril of the Peak*. He is sometimes called Edward, and sometimes Edmund Christian. He was one of the Christians of Ballakilley in Kirk Maughold, and of one of the oldest and most important families in the Isle of Man. The family was established in the Isle of Man so early as 1422 (see Hutchinson's *History of Cumberland*, vol. iii., p. 146). They had previously been established in Wigtownshire. There is apparently some error in Hutchinson's genealogy of the family of this Edward Christian, who is mentioned by Chaloner. He says: "1st brother, John, born 1602; 2nd, died young; 3rd, William, born 1608; 4th, Edward, Lieutenant-Governor of the Isle of Man, in 1629" (according to Sacheverell, *Manx Society*, vol. i., p. 78, in 1628). Now as the birth of the Edward, mentioned by Hutchinson, cannot be placed earlier than 1609, he could not well have made a fortune in the Indies, have frequented the court of Charles the First, and have been selected as a fit person to be a Lieutenant-Governor of the Isle of Man, in 1628, when he was only at the age of 19 or 20. It is probable that Hutchinson has confounded Edward Christian, with the Deemster, Edward Christian, of Ronaldsway, Deputy-Governor, in 1634. The person mentioned in the text, and in Peck's *Desiderata Curiosa*, was obviously of mature age. He appears to have been the brother of the William Christian, who married the heiress of Knock Rushen, near Castletown; and who, as well as Edward, was imprisoned in Peel Castle, in 1643. The mention of him by the Earl of Derby, in his letter to his son, contained in Peck's *Desiderata Curiosa* (given in vol. iii. *Manx Society*), is in the following terms: "I was newly got acquainted with Captain Christian, whom I perceived to have abilities enough to do me service; I was told he had made a good fortune in the Indies and that he was a Manxman born. He is excellent good company; as rude as a sea captain should be; but refined as one that had civilized himself half a year at Court, when he served the Duke of Buckingham. While he governed here some few years, he pleased me very well. But such is the condition of Man, that most will have some fault or other to blur all their best virtues; his was of that condition which is reckoned with drunkenness, viz., *covetousness*, both marked with age to increase and grow in man. When a prince has given all, and the favourite can desire no more, they both grow weary of one another."

From various documents we gather that Edmund or Edward Christian or Christin, was sentenced in 1643, by the Earl of Derby, to be imprisoned and pay a fine of 1000 marks. His true offence is presumed to have been the imprisonment of the Lord's Steward of the Abbey Lands, for an unlawful exaction of tithe. But it is evident from the Earl of Derby's letter to his son, that he was regarded as a person disaffected towards the Government, and a fomenter of treason, whom it was desirable to put out of the way. The family of the Christians (the Earl observes "Christins, for that is the true name") had made themselves chief in the Isle of Man, and occupied the most important posts; they were evidently Puritanically affected, and probably were the parties to whom the Earl alludes in the following terms (see vol. iii., *Manx*

Society, p. 35): "They were the principal disturbers of the peace, and such as we could prove to have incited others, and given them that dangerous oath and covenant after the manner of some other countries, which hath got us dear experience." It was a dangerous experiment, however, to lay upon Edward Christian so heavy a fine as 1000 marks, more especially as the Earl points to covetousness as the besetting sin of the family. Herein we are forced to admit that he lacked his ordinary discretion, and acted contrary to the advice he has given his son. "I remember one said it was safer much to take men's lives than their estates; for, their children will sooner much forget the death of their father, than the loss of their patrimony."

Probably the Earl would have taken Christian's life, if he could have done so on legal grounds; for he complains that the "judges did pretend that they wanted precedents" for his so doing. "God willing," writes he, "I will have laws declared for treason, and the like."

He continued in prison till 1651, when he was released by Colonel Duckenfield. In 1660, after the Restoration, he was remanded to Peel Castle, but was permitted, as an indulgence, to plead to a suit relative to property, in September, 1660; after which, he was sent back to prison, where he died at the beginning of the following year. [A copy of two of his autographs, in the years 1628 and 1632, taken from documents in Rushen Castle, are given in my story of *Rushen Castle and Rushen Abbey*.—Edit.] For a general account of his proceedings, reference must be made to vol. iii., *Manx Society*,—"Earl of Derby's Letter to his son." The following entry occurs in the register of Kirk Maughold, in the Isle of Man; the date, however, should be read 1660-61. "Edmund Christian sum time Captain at ye sea, and afterwards for a time Governour of ye Isle of Man, departed this life in ye Peel Castle, being a prisoner there for sum words spoken concerning ye king (Charles the First), when the great difference was betwixt King and Parliament. He was committed by James, Earl of Derby, being then in this Isle, and John Greenhalgh, Governour; and afterwards buried in Kirk Maughold Church, where he was baptised. Was buried January ye 22nd, 1660.",—(See Feltham's MS. Inscriptions.)

Note 17.—"Possibly may ensue thereof."

The Isle of Man is one of the richest, if not *the* richest, mining districts in the British Isles; yielding as much as 2,600 tons of lead ore, 3,181 tons of blend (sulphuret of zinc), 350 tons of copper, and 1,650 tons of hematite iron ore, in the year. The lead ore of Foxdale contains a very large per centage of silver, said to amount in some parts to upwards of 100 oz. per ton of lead ore: the total produce of silver from the Isle of Man, is now as much as 57,000 oz. per annum.—(See *Reports of the Mining Record Office*,) The chief mining districts for lead, are Foxdale and Laxey. Lead and copper are both found at Laxey and Brada (the Mine-hough, of the text). The latter district is that to which earliest attention was drawn; before the present century the former two were hardly worked. John Comyn, Earl of Buchan, obtained from Edward the First, in 1292, a licence to dig for lead in the Calf of Man (which may be regarded as part of the Brada district), to cover eight towers of his castle at Cruggleton, in Galloway.—(See The *Caledonia*, vol. iii., p. 372.) In the statute book of the Isle of Man, various notices of mining operations occur, under the dates A.D. 1422, 1613, 1618, 1630.,—See also *General View of the Agriculture of the Isle of Man*, by Thos. Quayle, Esq., 1812. In the workings at Brada, have been found a description of wedge, called feather-wedges, which were used before the introduction of gunpowder, indicating the earlier character of the works there carried on. A level appears to have been driven in near high-water mark, in the north-western face of Brada Head, for a distance of about 200 yards; and 36 feet above this a second adit was made, inclining downwards upon the vein whence a considerable quantity of lead ore was obtained. The present works are very much further inland, and go by the name of the "South Manx" Mines. But they are on part of the same system of veins as those which were earlier worked at Brada, or the "Mine-hough" of Chaloner.

Note 18.—"Extraordinary High Winds."

Sacheverell, as well as Chaloner, notes the violent winds oftimes occurring in the Isle of Man. But though the climate is windy, the annual amount of rain-fall is not excessive. In point of temperature, the Isle of Man is more equable than the Isle of Wight. Observations taken four times daily at Ballasalla, near Castletown, by J. Burman, Esq., F.R.A.S., for a period of seven years, give a difference of hardly more than 15 deg. Farenheit between the mean summer and winter temperatures. The difference between the mean summer and winter temperatures of the Isle of Wight is 24 deg. At the same time, we observe that the mean annual temperature of the Isle of Man is the highest, for the same latitude, of any place in Europe, being, according to the tables of Professor Dove of Berlin, 49.84 deg., or nearly 50 Farenheit. These remarks apply to the towns on the coast, and to the inland valleys. On the tops of the mountains, the cold is necessarily more severe; but even there, frost and snow are of comparatively rare occurrence.

Note 19.—"And although the same hath."

An anacolouthon: the text of this long sentence is extremely complicated; the drift of it being that the "Learned, Hospitable, Painful, and Pious Prelate Dr. Philips," was the better able to preach in Manx, and translate the Bible and

Prayer Book into that language, from its great affinity with his native Welsh. Reference is made to these labours of Bishop Philips, in the report of the "Society for Promoting Christian Knowledge" 1764; and it is stated that his translations never appeared in print. A "narrative of the origin, progress, and completion of the Manx version of the Holy Scriptures, and other religious books, for the use of the native inhabitants of the Isle of Man," is given in the appendix to the memoirs of Bishop Hildesly, by the Rev. Weedon Butler, 1799, pp. 211-360. The Manx Prayer Book was first printed in 1765; and the Bible in 1772.

For the points of resemblance between the Manx and the Welsh languages, reference may be made to the "Practical Grammar of the Antient Gaelic or language of the Isle of Man, usually called Manx," by the Rev. John Kelley, LL.D., originally printed in quarto, in 1804, and re-printed by the *Manx Society*, in their second volume, under the able editorship of the Rev. W. Gill, Vicar of Malew.—(See note 32 infra.)

Note 20.—"Sir."

On page 16 infra, Chaloner states "The Ministers who are Natives have alwaies this addition of Sir, unless they be Parsons of their parish." In Brydson's *Heraldry*, p. 175, it is said that when the Clergy Priests bore the titie of "Sir," it was as "the Pope's Knights." A title thus employed judicially, and declared as characterising the Pope's Knights, appears to have had some other foundation than mere courtesy. It was about the same period in like manner applied to the Monks, the proprietors of Cross-Ragwell Abbey. Sir Adam Fergusson (1795), had in his possession a copy of a testamentary deed, dated MD.XXX, wherein a number of Monks, to whom it relates, have the title Sir (dominus) prefixed to their names. We also find in *Heraldic Anomalies*, vol. i., p. 77, that in ancient times "Sir" was a common title of the Clergy, at least of the inferior order, being the regular translation of Dominus, the designation of those who had taken their first degree in the University. Hence, we have in Shakespear, Sir Hugh, in the "Merry Wives of Windsor"; Sir Topas, in "Twelfth Night"; Sir Oliver, in "As you like it"; and Sir Nathaniel, in "Love's Labour Lost." But that this title was quite distinct from Knighthood, is plain from what Viola says in "Twelfth Night"—"I am one that had rather go with *Sir Priest* than *Sir Knight.*"

It would appear from some old writings, that *Sir John* was often used as a soubriquet for an illiterate priest: apposite instances are cited by Mr. Albert Way, in his notes on the name John, in the *Prompter Parsed*, vol, i., p. 264. (P.B.)

Sir may, however, be a translation of the older form *Magister*, We read in the charter of Harald, King of Man, in 1246, "Magister Thomas de Mann"; "Magister Maurice clericus domini Regis de Mann."

Note 21.—"Sir Hugh Cavoll."

This is no doubt a misprint in the original text, for Sir Hugh Cannell, mentioned on page 17 infra, as assistant to Bishop Philips, in translating the Bible into Manx. He was many years Vicar of Michael Parish, having been appointed thereto about 1609; and died in 1670. Along with Sir W. Norris, Vicar-General, and his official Sir Wm. Crow, he was nominated by Bishop Philips in a commission for managing the ecclesiastical affairs of the diocese, during the Bishop's absence, on the 10th May, 1626. In May, 1610, he was present at a Convocation held in the Church of St. Patrick, in Holme (the Islet on which the Cathedral at Peel is situated), by the above Bishop. He was the father of that Deemster John Cannell (appointed in 1645), who is supposed to have connived at the Earl of Derby's proceedings in the matter of the "tenure of the straw." His grandson, Hugh Cannell, was Water-Bailiff of the Isle of Man, (whose mother was a daughter of Thos. Heskett, Esq., of North Wales,) who married Margaret, only daughter of Robert Calcott, Esq., of the Nunnery, near Douglas. The daughter and sole heiress of this latter Hugh Cannell, married Peter Heywood, Esq., Attorney-General of the Isle of Man, and so conveyed the Nunnery estate into that family. (P.B.) The first connection of the Heywoods with the Isle of Man, appears to have arisen from the circumstance that Alice, the daughter of the celebrated John Greenalgh, of Brandlesome, who maintained tranquility in the Isle of Man, as Governor, under James, Seventh Earl of Derby, from 1640 to 1651, becoming the widow of Theophilus Holt, of Grizzlehurst (by whom she was progenetrix on one side of the family of the Garretts, of Ballabroie, in Lezayre), married Peter Heywood, of Heywood, Lancashire; by whom she had issue two sons, Robert and Peter, and five daughters, Margaret, Martha, Jane, Elizabeth, and Dorothy. Robert, the eldest, became Governor of the Isle of Man, in 1678, and died January, 1690. He was interred in St. Mary's Church, Castletown; and removed in July, 1699, to the Parish Church of Malew: aged 57 years. Margaret married John Garrett, of Ballabroie, the third of that name in possession of Ballabroie, through whom, in another line, the Garretts trace their pedigree to the Heywoods and Greenhalghs. The youngest son, Peter, became connected with the Cannells in the way we have seen above.

On a brass, in the chancel of Lezayre Church, we read the following inscription:—"Here lyeth interred the body of Mrs. Margaret, daughter to Peter Heywood, of Heywood, in the Countie of Lancaster, Esq., by his wife Alice, daughter of John Greenalgh of Brandelsom, in the same Countie, Esq., and Governor of this Isle of Man many years; She was wife to Captain John Garrett, of Sulby, and left issue by him one sonne and three daughters, viz., John, Mary, Alice, Elizabeth; and died Jan. 16, and buried the 19th, A.D. 1669."

Annexed to this is another brass plate, bearing the inscription:—"The above John Garrett, Captain of Sulby, died 1692, aged 29 years; also his grand-daughter-in-law, Elizabeth, daughter of William Sutcliffe, of Stansfield Hall, within Halifax vicarage, by his wife, Grace Gibson, of Briggoyd, wife of John Garrett, the fifth of Ballabroie; died 13th March, 1745, aged 40 years; with four of her children, who died in their minority; and left issue Elizabeth, Ann, Margaret, Philip, William, Evan, and Alice."

Note 22.—"Latine and Greek."

Of the words which seem to have been derived from Latin and Greek, some are Ecclesiastical terms, as *agglish*, "the church"; *corpus annym*, "body and soul." Others may, like many words in the Welsh, have come from the Sanscrit, the corresponding Greek words having a like derivation. Sacheverell, (see vol. i., *Manx Society*, p. 15,) observes the resemblance of many Manx expressions to Latin, instancing *Qui fer a tye*, for *Qui vir tecti*. But *Qui fer a tye* as written by Sacheverell, *is not Manx*. Probably he meant *Quoi fer y thie*; which, however, is hardly grammatical. With respect to *thie*, "a house," we may doubt whether it be derived from the Latin *tectum* (*tego*, "I cover"); seeing that in the cognate Celtic languages, we have the same word in various shapes, as *tŷ*, "a house," in Welsh, *tigh*, in Gaelic; and the old British still seems preserved in the modern English *pigsty*, which is *pig's thie*, "the pig's house."

Note 23.—"Few speak the English Tongue."

The Manx, as a spoken language, now seems likely to share the fate of the Cornish, and in a few years it may perhaps be written "Few speak the Manx Tongue," as the Rev.

W. Gill observes, (*Manx Society*, vol. ii., p. 9,) "It is a doomed language—an iceberg floating in southern latitudes." The good service done to literature, by the *Manx Society*, in the re-publication of Dr. Kelly's *Manx Grammar*, in the contemplation of this event, becomes more and more evident, It is much to be hoped that the work of the Society, in printing also Dr. Kelly's *Triglott Dictionary*, may meet with sufficient encouragement, in order that philologists of future ages, may have within easy reach the means of investigating and comparing the extinct languages of the British Isles.

Note 24.—"And placed a Bishop there."

See note 87, p. 83, vol. i., *Manx Society*. Chaloner has wisely avoided the legend of Capgrave (alluded to by Sacheverell), of one Mordaius, King of Man, said to have been converted to Christianity in the first century, and the statement of Hector Boetius, followed by Bishop Spotiswood, that "Cratilinth, the Scottish King (A.D. 277), was very earnest in the overthrow of Druidism in the Isle of Man and elsewhere; and upon the occasion of Diocletian's persecution, when many Christians fled to him for refuge, he gave them the Isle of Man for their residence, and erected there for them a stately temple, called 'Sodorense Fanum,' and wherein Amphibalus, a Briton, sat first Bishop." The story of the Sodorense Fanum is further improved upon in Gibson's *Camden*, 1695, p. 1061, where it is said "The chief town [of the Isle of Man.—EDIT.] is Russin, situated towards the north side [really the south side.—EDIT.] of the Island, which, from a castle and garrison in it, is commonly called Castletown; where, within a little Isle, Pope Gregory the Fourth erected an Episcopal See, the Bishop whereof, named Sodorensis (from the Island as it is believed), had formerly jurisdiction over all the Hebrides." Hence, also, some have presumed that St. Michael's Isle, a little Isle adjoining the Promontory of

Langness, near Castletown, was the ancient Sodor. The error has probably originated from the circumstance that the little Isle near Peel, on the north side, on which was built a castle and cathedral, was in later years called Sodor. The Bishopric of Sodor, (Norse *Sudoer*, i.e., the "Southern Islands," thirty in number; the Orkneys and Shetland Islands being the *Nordoer*, or "Northern Islands,") of which the Episcopal Seat was in Iona, was not constituted by Pope Gregory the Fourth till 838; *i.e.*, 391 years after the institution of the Bishopric of Man, by St. Patrick. The Bishoprics of Man and Sodor were united at the beginning of the 11th century, and so continued till near the close of the 14th—about 300 years—when the Bishoprics were again separated; the Bishop of Man still claiming his ancient title of Bishop of Sodor and Man. It seems most improbable that if the conversion of the Manx to Christianity had occurred in the first century, they, themselves, should have no tradition of so remarkable an event. On the other hand, their conversion by St. Patrick is interwoven with all their earliest records and traditions.

Note 25.—"One Macfil, alias Maguil or Machalilus."

The name of this early Bishop of Man has been variously written Machutus, Macfield, Machilda, Machaldus, Magharde, and Maughold. The derivation of the name will perhaps be found in "Machaldus," contrasted with Ma-lew (St. Lupus), and Ma-rown (St. Rooney), both parishes in the Isle of Man where *Ma* signifies "Saint": Was *Ma-ckaldus* a "Culdee Saint"? The old legend is that he was an Irish robber or freebooter, converted by St. Patrick, by whose advice he committed himself manacled, in a coracle (or small wicker boat covered with hides), upon the waters of the Irish Sea, and was driven by the winds and currents upon the shores of the Isle of Man, near the promontory which still bears his name. The Church erected there in his honor, was ever held in great repute; and its precincts were a sanctuary for the Island. St. Maughold was chosen Bishop in 498.

Note 26.—"Of the Ancient Bishops."

On the death of St. Maughold, A.D. 518, St. Lomanus, a nephew of St. Patrick, succeeded to the Bishopric. After him were St. Conaghan and St. Rooney. From the above four Bishops, the following Manx Parishes received their names: Kirk Maughold, Kirk Lonnan (anciently Loman), Kirk Conchan, and Kirk Marown.

Note 27.—"The rest of the Western Isles."

It will be seen that whilst Chaloner adopts the idea of a town *Sodor*, placing it not in Man but in Iona, he nearly hits the truth by saying that in St. Columb's Isle "there had been anciently a Bishop's Seat, for that and the rest of the "Western Isles," (or Hebrides, which the Norwegians included under the name of the *Sudoer*.)—(See above, note 24.)

Note 28.—"And had his eyes put out."

Chaloner appears to have been led astray here by Matthew Paris, who has confounded Hamond, son of Jole, a Manxman, and first Bishop of Sodor and Man, with the atrocious Wymond, a Monk of Sais or Sees, in Normandy; who, in his own person, united the characters of a "Bishop, warrior, and freebooter"; and who was mutilated and deprived of his eyes, "not for the kingdom of heaven's sake," but for the peace of Scotland.—(See Oliver's *Monumenta, Manx Society*, vol. iv,, p. 227.)

Note 29.—"John, a Monk of Sais."

The place, (Sais, in Normandy,) is not printed in the original copy of Chaloner. John was consecrated in 1151, by Henry Mc Murdock, Archbishop of York; but as the date of

Hamond's death is not given in the *Chronicon Manniae*, there is room for believing that John may not have *immediately* succeeded Hamond; but that one, if not more Bishops intervened. There is also good reason for concluding that Eudo de Sourdeval, who was Abbot of Fumess, between 1134 and 1145, became Bishop of Sodor and Man, between Hamond and John. Documents are preserved (Harl. MSS., 1808, p. 67), printed in vol. vii., *Manx Society*, p. 7, one entitled "Recognitio Olavi Regis Mannie et Insularum," the other entitled "Littera Regis Insularum" (Chartæ Miscellaniae and ex Registro de Ecclesia Ebor, office of Duchy of Lancaster, *Manx Society*, vol. vii., p. 4), in which Olave Kleining (Olave the Dwarf), by the Grace of God King of the Isles, entreats Thurstan, Archbishop of York, to consecrate the Bishop who had been elected from amongst the inmates of Furness Abbey, and the Lord Abbot Eudo declares that he "neither would nor could go to any other person than the Archbishop of York."

Should it be the case that this Eudo was Bishop of Sodor and Man, between Hamond and John, the difficulty in reconciling dates, expressed by myself in vol. i., *Manx Society*, note 90, p. 87, will be removed.

Bishop John of Sais was buried 1160, in the Isle of St. Patrick, near Peel, where the Cathedral of St. German was afterwards built, of which Simon, who was Bishop of Sodor and Man from 1236 to 1247, erected the choir, and himself was buried there in 1247, having died on Feb. 23 of that year, according to the *Chronicon Manniae*.

Note 30.—"Consecration in Norway."

There was a constant struggle between York and Drontheim for the consecration of the Bishops of Sodor and Man, arising doubtless from the peculiar union of the two Sees, originally separated. At the beginning, the Bishops of

Man appear to have been consecrated by the Archbishop of
York. Shortly after the union of the two Sees, Olave, King of
Man, granted in A.D. 1134, by a charter (see Oliver's
Monumenta, Manx Society, vol. vii., p. 1) to "the Church of
the blessed Mary of Furness" the liberty of electing a "Bishop
of the Isles." We have seen (note 29 above), that Eudo (the
Bishop whom we have presumed to have been then elected),
states that he would not go to any other than the Archbishop
of York for consecration. His immediate successors, John and
Gamaliel, were consecrated at York; but in 1181, Reginald,
who was a Norwegian, of the royal family of Man, was
consecrated by the Archbishop of Drontheim. Also, Nicholas
de Meaux, Abbot of Furness (who was nominated by Olave
the Black, whilst his illegitimate brother Reginald was
usurping the throne of Man), was consecrated in 1193, at
Drontheim. Yet, in the first instance, application appears to
have been made on his behalf, in 1193, to the Archbishopric
of York.—(See *Littera Regis Insularum Directa Capitulo
Eborum pro Electo suo:. Cott. MSS.*, printed in Oliver's
Monumenta, Manx Society, vol. vii., p. 49.) And Nicholas calls
himself Bishop of the Isles, A.D. 1193, in a document
addressed "Omnibus sancte Matris Ecelesie filiis salutem,"
printed in vol. vii., *Manx Society*, p. 19, from the *Chartae
Miscellaniae*, Duchy Office,—(see also *Cott. MSS., Claudius*,
book iii., p. 131 b.), and states that his election had taken
place at the hands of the Monks of the Church of Holy Mary,
of Furness, to whom the right of election belonged, and who
had unanimously agreed to the election of this person.
Through the opposition of Reginald, it would seem that the
consecration sought for at York, was not obtained; and even
after Nicholas's consecration at Drontheim, he could not get
possession of his diocese, in consequence of which, in a letter
addressed by Pope Honorius the Third, in 1224, to the
Archbishop of York, we learn that he applied to the Pope, to

be permitted to relinquish his charge. Again, we know that
Simon was consecrated in 1236, by Peter, Archbishop of
Drontheim, at Bergen, in Norway. His successor, Lawrence,
was also consecrated in Norway, in 1249. Richard, who
followed him, was consecrated at Rome, in 1235, by the
Archbishop of Drontheim. After the Scottish conquest of
Man, during their occupation of it, all the Bishops were
consecrated in Norway; but after the English, under Sir
William Montacute, in 1343, finally got possession of the Isle,
the intercourse with Norway was cut off. William Russel, in
1348, was consecrated by the Cardinal Bishop of Ostia; and
John Donkan, a Manxman, Archdeacon of Down, Collector
of Papal Revenues, and last true Bishop of *Sodor and Man*,
was elected by the Clergy of Man, at Peel Cathedral, on the
Feast of Corpus Christi, 1374, confirmed by Pope Gregory
the Eleventh, October 15, and was consecrated at Avignon,
Nov. 15, of the same year, by Simon Langham, afterwards
Archbishop of Canterbury. It is somewhat singular that the
first and last Bishop of the true Diocese of *Sodor and Man*,
was a native of the Isle of Man; and there has been no
Manxman Bishop, since John Donkan.

Note 31.—"The First Bishop that was Consecrated and
Confirmed by the Pope."

See the end of previous note. The Papal power culminated
in the Isle of Man under John Donkan. After the separation
of the Dioceses, the liberties of the Church were greatly
curtailed, more particularly under the Lordship of Sir John
Stanley the Second, who anticipated in Man, by 100 years,
the assertion of the supremacy of the crown, made by Henry
the Eighth.

Henceforth, the Bishops of Man became the mere
nominees of the Lord of the Isle; and in their election, the
clergy and people took no part. At the present time, there

is not even a Dean and Chapter to whom, as in England, the crown makes the sham of a choice in the appointment of a Bishop.

The Bishops, succeeding John Donkan, up to the time of Bishop Philips, next mentioned by our author, were:—

Robert Welby or Waldby, of Aire, in Gaacony   ........A.D. 1380

John Sprotton 1400

John Burgelin, a Franciscan 1425

Richard Pulley 1429

John Greene 1449

Thomas Burton, a Franciscan 1455

Thomas of Kirkham 1459

Richard Oldham, Abbot of Chester 1480

Huan, or John Hesketh (probably Bishop till 1542) 1487

Thomas Stanley (son of Sir Ed. Stanley), deprived 1545 1542

Robert Ferrar or Ferrier (translated to St. David's) 1546

Henry Mann (Dean of Chester) 1546

Thomas Stanley restored (Sword Bishop) 1556

John Salisbury, Dean of Norwich 1569

James Stanley, (?) son of Lord Monteagle 1573

John Merrick (Sword Bishop) 1577

George Lloyd (translated to Chester, in 1604) 1600

John Philips, Dean of Cleveland. Philips died in 1633, ...1605
and was buried in Peel Cathedral.

After Philips, came William Foster, in 1633, who died in 1635; to whom succeeded Richard Parr, in the same year. On his death, which took place in 1643, the See was kept open for 17 years, when Samuel Rutter was insltalled in Peel Cathedral, Oct. 8th, 1660.

In my notes to Sacheverell's *Short Survey of the Isle of Man*, (*Manx Society*, vol. i.,) on p. 181, I alluded to a remarkable silver bracelet, which was dug up in 1855, in a garden near Rathmines, Dublin, and at that time, 1859, in possession of

Captain Edward Hoare, of the Cork Rifles, and bearing an inscription which indicated that it once belonged to a Thomas, Bishop of Man. The legend, on this remarkable relic, is "S. Thome Dei Gratia Episcopi Mannensis." But the question is, to which of the Thomases, Bishops of Man (for there were several), it belonged. My reference to it was given under the name of Thomas, consecrated at Drontheim, Norway, A.D. 1334. In the above list of Manx Bishops, we have two Thomases, the latter of whom immediately succeeded the former; *viz.*, Thomas Burton, Bishop in 1455, and Thomas of Kirkham, Bishop in 1459; to one of whom, from the character and style of workmanship, the bracelet seems rather to have belonged, than to the Thomas of 1334.

Miss Wilks, of Douglas, grand-daughter of Vicar-General Wilks, who has devoted herself much to the study of Manx antiquities, in a remarkable memoir upon this relic, with a sight of which she has favored me, has pointed out several facts tending to the conclusion that Thomas Burton was its original owner. She says, "Bishop Burton was a near connection of Sir Edward Burton, of York, the personal friend of Edward the Fourth, fighting with him 15 battles, and made a Knight Banneret on the field of battle at St. Alban's, A.D. 1460. Two brothers, Burton, of the Longnor family, emigrated to Dublin in 1610, probably in reduced circumstances, for we find one of them a Banker, and afterwards advanced to the Corporation honor of Lord Mayor—as were also his sons, one of them, the ancestor of Sir William Burton, of Burton Hall, and of Pollarton, county Carlow. The noble house of Conyngham, now also claims descent through them, from the valiant soldier, Sir Edward Burton. In 1855, this silver bracelet was dug up at Rathmines; of which place, all that concerns this matter is, that there never was a monastery there, but several castles, and that of Rathmines was formerly the country residence of the Lords

Lieutenants of Ireland; the ground is still called the *bloody field*, being the site of a battle fought between the Duke of Ormondes forces and the army of Cromwell, commanded by General Jones, in 1649."

From the connection of the Burton family with Dublin, Miss Wilks argues that this bracelet, an heir loom of the family, may have been conveyed thither on the emigration of the two brothers from Longnor, in 1610. The bracelet (if it be such in reality), was described in the Journal of the *Archaeological Institute of Great Britain and Ireland*, in No. 56, 1857, vol xiv., pp. 365-6, and in No. 59, 1858, vol. xv., p. 289. It was purchased at the sale of the collection of Captain Edward Hoare, in 1861, and was exhibited by Mr. W. H. Forman, at a Meeting of the *British Archaeological Institute*, in 1861, of which the following notice occurs in the *Athenaeum* for May:—"Mr. W. H. Forman exhibited a silver bracelet, with the impress of the seal of Thomas Burton, Bishop of Sodor and Man, 1452—1480, (1455—1480,— EDIT.,) found in a garden at Rathmines, near Dublin, Nov., 1855. This unique relic weighs 4 ozs. 7 dwts. The seal forming its front represents the mitred prelate giving the benediction with the right hand, and holding the pastoral staff in his left. He stands within a tabernacle, below which is an arch and a second representation of the Bishop, with hands uplifted in prayer. On the verge, is the legend 'S. Thome: Dei: Gratia: Episcopi: Mannensis.' It has an elegant foliated border; and the hooping has prominent scrolls and armlets, once probably set with jewels, or decorated with colored enamels."

Note 32.—"The first was Dr. Philips."

Dr. John Philips was a native of North Wales. Wood says (*Athen. Ox.*, vol. i., p. 629), that he received his academical education in Oxford; became afterwards Parson of Thorpe Basset and Slingsby, in Yorkshire, obtaining this latter in

March, 1591. He is the first Archdeacon mentioned in the
Archdeacon of the Isle of Man's books, as appointed to the
Archdeaconry of Man, in 1587. About 1590, he became
Chaplain to Henry, Earl of Derby. In April, 1601, he was
made Archdeacon of Cleveland. He was also Rector of
Harwarden, in Flintshire. On the translation, of Dr. Lloyd,
Bishop of Sodor and Man, to the Bishopric of Chester, in
1605 (according to Willis 1604), Dr. Philips became his
successor in Man: Wood says not till 1614. He is supposed
to have held the Archdeaconry of Cleveland and the
Rectory of Slingsby in commendam. He died August 7th,
1633; and was interred in the Cathedral Church of St.
German, at Peel. According to Sacheverell, he translated, or
caused to be translated into Manx, not only the Bible, but
also the Prayer Book. The latter though not printed, is noted
by Sacheverell as being extant in MS., in his day, but not the
Bible.—(See vol. i., *Manx Society*, p. 91.) This identical MS.
is now in the possession of Mrs. Newton, of Westham,
Castletown, who is the grand-daughter of Vicar-General
Wilks; and was exhibited by the Rev. W. Gill, the Vicar of
Malew, at a Meeting of the *Manx Society*, September 1st,
1863. Appended to it is the following note, by the late John
Mc' Hutchin, Esq., Clerk of the Rolls, in the Isle of Man:—
"It appears to have been written at an early period of the
reign of Charles the First; see the Litany, where
interlineations are made to suit the reign of Charles the
Second." In a letter from the Rev. W. Gill, Vicar of Malew,
to Paul Bridson, Esq., Honorary Secretary of the *Manx
Society*, he states that "on further examination of the MS.,
the date may be assigned to it between 1625 and 1630, as it
contains a prayer for Charles the First and his Queen Maria,
but not for their son; the son's name (Prince Charles, *i.e.*
Charles the Second), has been interlined; therefore, Charles
the First coming to the throne in 1625, and Charles the

Second being born in 1630, the Prayer Book must date
between these two periods." It is worth remarking that this
Prayer Book does not contain the clause in the Litany *as dy
chur er ash as dy hannaghtyn dooin bannaghtyn ny marrey*,
i.e., "and to restore and continue to us the blessings of the
sea;" and this circumstance gives good colour to the
tradition that the clause was inserted in the Manx Prayer
Book by Bishop Wilson.

The Manx Prayer Book properly contains no prayer for
the High Court of Parliament of Great Britain and Ireland;
but instead of it, is a prayer for the members of the House
of Keys (the Insular Legislature), together with a prayer for
the Lord and Lady of the Isle; as clauses in the Litany and
in the prayer for the Royal Family; *viz.*, *As maroosyn yn
Chiarn, yn Lady, as Fir-reill yn Ellan shoh*, i.e., "And with
them the Lord, the Lady, and Rulers of this Isle." These
clauses were so printed in the Manx Prayer Book of 1765;
their omission in the edition of 1840, is without authority.
The clause in the Litany for the blessings of the sea, though
not printed, is still always used in Manx or English, in the
churches of the Isle of Man. It is one of the few remaining
evidences of the independence of the Manx Church,
unfettered by an "Act of Uniformity."

Note 33.—"The other was Dr. Pabb, a Lancashire Man."

In the Registry of Burials, in the Parish of Ballaugh, Isle
of Man, under date 1644, is the following entry:—"Richard
Parr, Parson of Eccleston, in Lancashire, Lord Bishop of
Sodor and Man, departed this life the 23d of March, *att*
Bishop's Court, and was buried in Bishop Phillips' grave,
in the Cathedral Church within the Castle of Peele, the
26th March."

The following account of him is gathered from Baines's
History of Lancashire, vol. iii., p. 476; Wood's *Athenae*

Oxonienses, vol. ii., p. 6; and the xxii. vol. of the *Cheetham Societies Works*, entitled *Notitia Cestriensis*, part 3, p. 372.

Richard Parr, D.D., was born at Eccleston, Lancashire, in the year 1692. He entered as a Student at Brazen-nose College, Oxford, on the 2nd September, 1609. He was elected Fellow of his College in 1614, being then B.A. Afterwards proceeding in the same faculty, he entered into the Sacred Function, and became a frequent Preacher. In 1626, he was admitted to the reading of the sentences; and two years after, became Rector of Ludbrook, in Warwickshire, but resigning that living on being instituted to the Rectory of Eccleston, his native place, in 1628. He proceeded to the degree of D.D., in 1634; and in the subsequent year, 1635, was consecrated Bishop of Sodor and Man, holding Eccleston in commendam. The living of Eccleston was put under sequestration by the Parliament, and then it was given to Mr. Edward Gee, "an orthodox preaching Minister," together with a cornmill, valued at £30 per annum, and also other tithes. He died in 1644.

He published several sermons, all very scarce. His nephew, Edward Parr, of Parr's Wood, in Eccleston, married Margaret, daughter of Edward, and granddaughter of Richard Robinson, of Euxton, gent., and of his wife Margaret, daughter of Mr. Adam Holland, of Newton, near Manchester, a very near connection of Humfrey Chetham, of Turton, in Bolton-le-Moors, Esq. In a MS. in the possession of Paul Bridson, Esq., written in 1765, it is stated that Bishop Parr rebuilt the Chapel at Ramsey, anciently called the Trine of Ballure, and dedicated it to St. Catherine. (P. B.)

Note 34.—"Chappels in this Isle."

These Chapels (called Treen Chapels, and said to have been instituted by St. German), were originally 193 in number; *i.e.*, one to each four quarter-lands, or about 11 for each parish. For the origin and name of these Chapels, see vol. i., *Manx Society*, note 121, p. 93.

Note 35.—"Mr. Thomson, an Englishman."

A Mr. John Thompson appears Vicar of Kirk Christ Lezayre and Rushen, in 1660; and was succeeded in the latter living by a Richard Thompson, in 1680. (P. B.)

Note 36.—"A Rushy Bog."

Chaloner is not fortunate in his derivations, though assisted, as he says, by "Mr. Robert Parr, Parson." Sacheverell, in many instances, has copied him. "Kirk Christ Rushen," or "the Church of the Holy Trinity in Rushen," was so called from its being situated in the *Sheading of Rushen*, in distinction from "Kirk Christ Lezayre," the Church of the Holy Trinity, in the *Sheading of Ayre*. A Castle, an Abbey, and a Sheading, are named after St. Russin, who was one of the twelve Missionary fathers, who settled with St. Columba, in Iona, in 563. Again, Kirk Arbory is a corruption of Kirk Kerebre or Kirk Cairbre. In the old map accompanying this volume of Chaloner's, the parish is given under its true name, "Kirk Kerebrey." St. Cairbre was a disciple of St. Patrick: and in the Rotuli Scotiae, temp. Edward the First, we read of the "Church of St. Cairber, in Man."—(See *Manx Society*, vol. i., note 34, p. 14.) So also, in the Bull of Pope Eugenius the Third, to Furness Abbey, a.d. 1153, amongst the confirmation of grants in Man, to that Abbey, we read of "Terram sancti Carebrie."—(See vol. vii., *Manx Society*, p. 11.) Sacheverell and others state that the Parish Church of Arbory was dedicated in honor of St. Columba. It is somewhat singular, that in the declaration of the Bishop, Abbot, and Clergy in Man, against the claims of Sir Stephen Lestrop, (see vol. vii., *Manx Society*, p. 247,) the Church of Kirk Christ Rushen is called the Church of "the Holy Trinity in the fields" ("Michaelis canonicus vicarius ecclesio sancti Trinitatis de Ayre, Willielmus vicarius ecclesie sancti Trinitatis *inter prata*"). It is evident from its juxtaposition with Kirk Christ's Lezayre, that Kirk Christ's Rushen, is here intended; and the "inter prata" certainly looks very much like Chaloner's derivation "because built on the side of a Rushy bog"; and it is further countenanced by the fact that the lowlands about the Parish Church are Intack, not Quarterlands, from which we may infer that they were formerly not in a state of cultivation.

Kirk Braddan is derived from St. Brandanus or Brendinus, one of the early Bishops of Man; and Kirk Conchan, from St. Conaghan, also an early Bishop of the Isle. Kirk Malew is from St. Lupus, as appears by the inscription on an ancient paten, still preserved in that Church: "Sancte Lupe ora pro nobis." Kirk Marown is named from St. Rooney, an early Bishop of Man.

Note 37.—"Sir John Crelling."

In the *Episcopal Registry* (without date), is a petition from this Parish, signed by Richard Stevenson, Thos. Norris, Wm. Tyldesley, Charles Stanley, and sixty other subscribers, praying that Mr. Crelling, who has been with them eight years, may be presented with the said Vicarage. It is addressed to Richard Sherlock, B.D., and Samuel Hinde, B.D., "delegates for ecclesiastical affairs in the Isle." These two clergymen were appointed during the vacancy in the Bishopric, by Charles, Eighth Earl of Derby, who succeeded to the title in 1651, on the execution of his father at Bolton, for settling the ecclesiastical affairs of the Island. Mr. Crelling is set down as Vicar in 1650; but it is plain from the foregoing document, taken in connection with the time of appointment of the delegates, that such a date is too early. Probably the presentation was in 1658. (P. B.)

Note 38.—"Sir Thomas Parr, Minister."

He was instituted to this Vicarage in 1641, on the removal of Mr. Robert Parr to the Rectory of Ballaugh, and continued Vicar to 1691; and died in 1695. He was also a Surrogate. As Vicar of Malew, he appears as present at the festivities held in Castle Rushen, at Christmas, 1643-4, from the following singular document, which is signed by him:—"A.D. 1643. The Right Honble James, Earle of Derbie, and his Right Honble. Countess, invited all the Officers, Temporall and Spiritual, the Cleargie, the 24 Keyes of the Isle, the Crowners with all their wives, and likewise the best sort of the rest of the Inhabitants of the Isle, to a great majke (*mask?*), when the right honble. Charles, Lord Strange, with his traine, the right honble, Ladies wth their attendance, were most gloriously decked." (P. B.)

Note 39.—"Old Sir John Coshenham."

This "Sir John Cosnahan, Vicar of Kirk Santon, being Minister of the said parish 38 years, departed this life the 24th June, 1656, and was buried the next day following, in the yard under the Great Broad Stone, for he left in his last will that he should be buried there."—(*Parochial Register*; see also *Hildesley's Life*, p. 298.) (P. B.) The Great Broad Stone, as it is called, covers the remains of six clergymen of the name of Cosnahan, four of whom were Vicars of Santon. The following notice of the family of the Cosnahans is given in the handwriting of Bishop Thomas Wilson, in 1739. Referring to a John Cosnahan, who was Vicar-General, and died in 1749, he says:—"Above 200 years ago, one Cosnahan, supposed to have come from Scotland, arrived at Peel town, and settled there. He had issue three sons, for one of whom he bought an estate near Peel aforesaid, called Balla Moar. The other son he educated a Clergyman; the descendants of whom settled in Kirk Santon, and have been Vicars of that

Parish successively. The purchase of Balla Kelly made by them, is at present in the possession of John Cosnahan, who was heir to his father Hugh, who was heir to his father John, Vicar of the said Parish, the first purchaser of the estate of Balla Kelly."

The first Clergyman on record of the name of Cosnahan, is a John Cosnahan (written *Quislahan*), who was Vicar of Jurby, in 1675. (P. B)

Note 40.—"Sir William Coshenham."

He was Vicar of Kirk German, in 1621, and also within Peel Castle in 1653, when he was succeeded by Sir Thomas Harrison. (P. B.)

Note 41.—"Mr. Robert Parr, Parson."

There were three or four Robert Parrs, Ministers about this period: *viz.*, Robert Parr. Vicar of Arbory, in 1713; a Vicar of Malew, in 1653; a Rector of Ballaugh, in 1640 (the one mentioned in the text); a Robert Parr, Vicar-General, and also Vicar of Lezayre, in 1680, and still Vicar when the Church was rebuilt, in 1704; there was a Robert Parr, Rector of Kirk Bride, in 1723, where he was succeeded in 1729, by the Rev. W. Bridson. (P. B.)

Note 42.—"Sir. John Huddlestone, the present Curate."

In the Church Registry of Andreas, 1677, is the following entry:—"Sir John Christian was Curate after the death of Sir John Huddlestone, under Archdeacon Fletcher:" and at the head of the marriages, A.D. 1677, and amongst the baptisms of the same year, thus, "Sir John Huddlestone died this year (1677), and Sir John Christian succeeded as Curate in this Parish, under the Rev. Dr. W. Urquart, Archdeacon of this Isle, and Vicar of a Parish in Kent, near London." See also in Baines's *Lancashire*, a Latin epitaph, commemorative of

Fletcher, Archdeacon of Sodor and Man, who died 24th March, 1688, aged 73. (P. B.)

Note 43.—"Sir Edward Crow, Minister."

The testimony which Chaloner bears to the piety and talents of the Manx Clergy as a body, in his day, is extremely valuable. It is, however, somewhat singular, that though giving the names of all the other Clergy, he does not give that of Archdeacon Rutter; who, by virtue of his office, was also Rector of Andreas. He may have heen absent from the Island in attendance on the Derby family. When he mentions above, the Clergy of the different Parishes, giving the title of *Minister* to the Vicars, and *Parson* to the Rectors, under the head of Kirk Andreas, he puts down Sir John Huddlestone, *Curate.* For the character of Archdeacon Rutter, see Earl of Derby's letter to his son, *Manx Society,* vol. iii., pp. 41-42. "He was a man," wrote the Earl, "for whom you and I may both thank God." How entirely the son agreed with the Father in this opinion of Rutter may he learnt from the circumstance that at the Restoration he nominated him to the Bishopric: Rutter was installed Bishop of Man, at his Cathedral of Peel, October 8th, 1660, and occupied the See till his death, in 1668.

The title *Sir,* prefixed to the names of Vicars and Curates, but not of Rectors, by Chaloner, has been explained in note 20.

Note 44.—"Priory of Rushen."

For an account of the foundation of the Abbey of Rushen, see Oliver's *Monumenta,* in the iv. and vii. vols., *Manx Society,* where several charters and papers connected with this Abbey, as an offshoot from Furness, are given. Also see the *Story of Rushen Castle and Rushen Abbey,* by the Editor: Bell and Daldy, London.

Note 45.—"Friers Minors at Bimaken."

The Friary of Bimaken, Bemaken, or Bechmaken, in Kirk Arbory, belonged to the Order of Grey Friars, and was founded in 1373. The only portion of it which now remains is the Chapel, converted into a barn; the door and windows of which have a Third Pointed character. A short account of its effects and appurtenances (as well as those at the Nunnery at Douglas), at the period of its dissolution, 34, 35, 36 Henry the Eighth, is given in the Rolls at the Augmentation Office, Carlton Bide.—See *Story of Rushen Castle and Rushen Abbey*, p. 52; in the appendix to which work is given the "Computus" of the possessions of Rushen Abbey, made in the year 1541. In the original text of Chaloner, the name is misprinted *Brinnaken*.

Note 46.—"Revenue upon the Ministers."

The character of Lord Fairfax in this respect, stands out in the highest colours, and seems to have given rise to the present position of the Clergy of the Isle of Man. Prior to 1839, the value of the Vicarages of the Isle of Man was miserably small; the large tithes being taken by the Bishop and the Crown, which had purchased them along with his remaining rights in the Island, from John, Fourth Duke of Athol, the Lord of the Isle in 1825. In the year 1839, the Crown, the Bishops, and the Clergy agreed to commute the several tithes payable to them, for the sum of £5,575 (regulated from year to year by the price of corn); and a re-distribution of the sum total was made in the following proportions:—

The Incumbents of Parishes	£3292 12 0
The Lord Bishop	1516 0 0
The Crown	525 0 0
Chaplain of St. Jade's, Andreas	101 0 0
Trustees of the Clergy Widows' Fund ...	1418 0 0
	£5675 0 0

The incomes of the Vicars were thus raised to £141.8s.0d. each, exclusive of their glebes. The Rectors of Ballaugh and Bride, £303.0s.0d. each; and the Archdeacon, £707.0s.0d.

Note 47.—"The Bishops have been persons of singular piety."

This testimony is particularly worthy of note, as shewing the discernment of the Earls of Derby in their choice of Bishops, and the deep interest which they took in the spiritual welfare of the Isle, committed to their trust. "Have this in your thoughts first," says James, Seventh Earl of Derby, in his famous letter to his son, preserved in Peck's *Desiderata Curiosa*, "to choose a reverend and holy man to your Bishop, who may carefully see the whole Clergy do their duties." The injunction was attended to by this son and grandson, so that the Bishops of the next 50 years and more, were not in any way inferior to those of the previous 50, commended by Chaloner. To the names of Philips, Foster, and Parr, of the 50 years before Chaloner's eulogium, must be added those of Rutter, 1660; Dr. Isaac Barrow, 1668 (the true founder of King William's College, Castletown); Henry Bridgman, 1671; Dr. Lake (afterwards translated to Chester, and one of the seven Bishops confined in the Tower by James the Second), 1682; Baptist Levinz, 1685; and last, but not least, the Apostolic Thomas Wilson, 1698, who was Bishop of Sodor and Man for 57 years.

Note 48.—"The proving of Wills."

During the Commonwealth, the proving of wills was vested in the Civil Magistrates, who instituted a Court called the Willer's Court, which ceased to exist in 1660. The following is a true copy of a summons served by Chaloner himself, who received his appointment as Governor under Lord Fairfax, in 1669:—

"Duglas, ye 23d July, 1659.

You are hereby required to meet at St. John's Chappell, on ye 26th day of this instant Month, about the proving of Mrs. Parr, late deceased, her will, without fail.

JAMES CHALONER."

To Capt. Stevenson and
Mr. William Quayle,   "To Capt. Stevenson, of
Judges of the Will Court."   Balladoole, These."

We find the following statement in some notes taken from the mouth of Vicar-General John Harrison, Dec. 12, 1678, in an inquiry by Bishop Henry Bridgman, in presence of his Registrar, Mr. Richard Fox, Clerk:—"The Parliament Power made Lay Officers, which they named 'Willers,' one while Mr. Samuel Radcliffe and Captain John Teare, who had registers, William Christian, Mr. Patrick Cannell, and Edward Brew, all persons of very mean judgment, who defaced much the records and kept them in very base order, which cannot yet be repayred. Within three years next after, succeeded Major Richard Stevenson (see above,) and Mr. W. Quayle, as Willers, and Mr. Thomas Norris, Registr, who kept their proceedings in very good order, and continued until the happy Restoration." (P. B.)

Note 49.—"Their said respective interests."

The Priors and Abbots of these different foundations, who were Barons of the Isle, were summoned as such by Sir John

Stanley, at the Hill of Reneurling, in 1422, to do fealty to him for their holdings; and not appearing, their possessions in the Isle were confiscated. These Ecclesastical Barons, holding lands in the Island but not living there, were the Prior of St. Ninians or St. Trinians, at Withorne, in Galloway; the Prior of St. Bede's, in Copeland (Cumberland); the Abbots of Banchor or Bangor and Sabal, in Ireland; and the Abbot of Furness, in Lancashire. Separate Courts for the Baronies are still held by the officers of the crown.—(See *Note* 67)

Note 50.—"Inhabited by the Ancient Scots."

It is the universal tradition that the earKer inhabitants of the Isle of Man were Scoto-Irish. The statement of Nennius is that "the Scots came from the parts of Spain to Ireland;" and "this people coming from Spain, gradually possessed many regions of Britain; and one Biule, with his followers, occupied Eubonia, that is Man, and other Islands round about. 'Buile autem cum suis tenuit Euboniam Insulam et alia circiter.'" It seems very doubtful, however, what the original name in Nennius, (or the author passing under his name,) may have been. Camden states, edition 1637, "Nennius hath written that one *Biule*, a Scot, was Lord of it (*i.e.*, Man)." On the other hand, Sacheverell writes (see vol. i., *Manx Society*, p. 24), "We are informed by Mr. Camden, out of Nennius, that the Island was conquered by one Binley, a Scot." It is very easy to see that such a name as Binle may be written so that a printer would be doubtful whether he should print it Builc, Biule, or Birle. Hence, may have originated the various names attributed in Nennius, Camden, Chaloner, and Sacheverell, to one and the same Manx Ruler. The Buile of Nennius, may be the same as the Birle mentioned by our author.

Note 51.—"Mannanan Mac Bar."

The Manx have a legendary ballad of the beginning of the 16th century, referring to this ancient ruler; and the statute book of the Isle of Man also makes mention of him in the following terms:—"Mannanan-Beg-Mac-y-Lheir (*i.e.*, Little Mannanan son of the sea), the first person who held Man, was the ruler thereof, after whom the land was named; he reigned many years, and was a paynim (*i.e.*, a *pagan*), that kept the Island under a mist, by his necromancy. If he dreaded an enemy, he could cause one man to seem a hundred, and that by magic art." He is said to have been converted to Christianity by St. Patrick.—(See Oliver's *Monumenta, Manx Society*, vol. iv., p. 84.) Perhaps our author's "Mannanan Mac Bar," is a misprint for *Mannanan Mac Lar* or *Mannanan Mac Leir*.

Note 52.—"Mona in Caesar and Tacitus."

Chaloner differs from most writers in stating that the Mona of Caesar was Anglesea. Caesar's words (*Comment - aries*, book v.), are "*In hoc medio cursu* est insula, quae appellatur Mona; "*i.e.*, *midway* between England and Ireland lies the Island called Mona. The expression "medio cursu," certainly seems more applicable to Man than to Anglesea. See the subject fully discussed in *A short dissertation about the Mona of Caesar and Tacitus*, by Mr. Thomas Brown, originally attached to Sacheverell's *Survey of the Isle of Man*, and printed in vol. i., *Manx Society*.

Note 53.—"Some enclosed in Coffins of Stone."

The Isle of Man is remarkable for the large number of barrows, cairns, cists, stone circles, and bauta-stones (*bauter steiner*), tall uninscribed stones, such as the two called the "giant's quoiting stones," near Port St. Mary; these latter are probably remains of the *Heathen* Northmen; the

Christianised Northmen afterwards erected Runic
monuments. The barrows and cairns may either be Norse or
Celtic, the few remains found in them not being of a
character sufficiently distinct to determine which.—(See vol.
i., *Manx Society*, note 47, p. 19; and *A Guide to the Isle of Man*,
by the Rev. J. G. Cumming, pp. 149, 150, 161; also see
"Worsaae's *Antiquities, &c.*)

Note 54.—"Were expulsed thence."

Edwin, King of Northumbria, following up his successes
against Cadwallon, A.D. 626, wrested the Isle of Man from the
Scots, who then were in possession of it. On the death of
Edwin, A.D. 633, in the battle of Heathfield, Cadwallon not
only regained his own territories, but gained also the Isle of
Man. It is stated by Bede, that when Cadwallon was slain at
Denisbrook, A.D. 636, King Oswald, and after him, in 642,
his brother Oswy, gained possession of the Nevanian Islands,
i.e., Man and Anglesea.

Note 55.—"Came under the Subjection of the Norwegians
by Conquest."

Chaloner passes entirely over the Norwegian occupation
of the Isle of Man, from 888 to 920; and its Danish Kings,
from 920 to 1066. The renowned Norwegian, Harald
Haarfagr, invaded the Isle of Man in 888, and overthrew
Anaraud, the last Welsh King; and left as his Viceroy, the Jarl
Ketil Bjornson, called also Flatnefr. In A.D. 890, Ketil declared
himself independent; and this line of rulers was continued
in Helgi and Thorstein, his son and grandson. On the
expulsion of Thorstein, in 894, according to the *Egilla Saga*,
one Nial or Neil was set upon the throne, and his nephew
Olave, succeeded him in 914. Then according to Manx
tradition came Orry or Erik, a Dane, who landed at the
Lhane River, in the north of the Island, from a strong fleet,

about 920. He was gladly received by the Manxmen, and established a line of Kings who have left permanent memorials of themselves. These were Guthred or Godred the First (who founded Rushen Castle, in 947), then Reginald the First; Olave the First; Olain; Allan; Fingal the First; Godred the Second; Macon or Hacon, in 973, son of Harold, King of Dublin (who was constituted High Admiral, by our Anglo-Saxon Edgar, and whose name appears in the Charter of Glastonbury); then Godred the Third; Reginald the Second; Suibne; Harold the First; Godred the Fourth; and Fingal the Second, in 1076. In Fingal the Second ended the Danish line; for Godred Crovan (the son of Harold the Black, of Iceland), who had fled to the Isle of Man in 1066, (when Harold Haardrardr, the Norwegian, was beaten by the Anglo-Saxon Harold, at Stanford Bridge), and had been there hospitably entertained by Fingal, subsequently in the year 1077, invaded the Isle of Man, with a great fleet from Norway; and overthrowing and slaying Fingal, in the battle of Sky-Hill, near Ramsey, gained possession of the throne of Man, and divided the Island amongst his followers. This dynasty lasted nearly 200 years; *i.e.*, till the conquest of the Island by the Scotch, in 1270. The conquest by Godred Crovan, was that conquest mentioned by Chaloner, in the text, as taking place in 1066. Godred Crovan reigned in Man 16 years; but in 1093, he was expelled from his kingdom by Magnus Nudipes, the Piratical King of Norway, and died in the Isle of Isla, in 1095. He left three sons—Lagman, Harold, and Olave: the first of whom, on the death of Magnus, in 1103, regained possession of his father's kingdom; but after a reign of 7 years, on account of his tyranny and cruelty, he was expelled by his subjects; and going on a pilgrimage to the Holy Land, died there. Olave, the youngest son of Godred Crovan, called also Olave Kleining, or the Dwarf, being then under age, a Regent was appointed for four years; but in 1114,

Olave, who had married Affreca, a grand-daughter of Henry
the First of England, was placed upon his father's throne, and
reigned till 1154, when his son, Godred the Black, succeeded
him. The table of the descendants of Godred the Black, is
given in *Appendix C.*

Note 56.—"This Isle the Scots held but 74 years."

This statement is not strictly correct. The Scotch, under
John Comyn and Alexander Stewart, of Paisley (according to
Sacheverell, see *Short Survey of the Isle of Man*, p. 55, vol. i.,
Manx Society), conquered the Manx in the battle of
Ronaldsway, October 8th, 1270. The King of Norway,
Magnus, ceded to Alexander the Third of Scotland, his right
and title to the Isle of Man and the Hebrides, in consideration
of 4,000 marks sterling, to be paid in four yearly instalments,
with a quit rent of 100 marks per annum, for ever, in a treaty
executed at Perth, in 1266. The Manx, under the instigation
of Ivar, the grandson of the Usurper Reginald, and son of
Godred Don (the same who in conjunction with his brother
Harold and others, had murdered King Reginald—son of
Olave the Black—in 1249—see *Appendix C*), declined this
transfer of their allegiance. On the arrival of the expedition
of the Scotch, under the conduct of John Comyn and
Alexander Stewart, at Derbyhaven, in the Isle of Man, the
Manx resisted the landing, and were utterly overthrown on
the field of Ronaldsway hard by, with the loss of their leader
Ivar, and 536 of their chief men. The battle happened on
October 8th, 1270. Alexander then placed over the Island a
succession of Governors: Godred Mc Manus; Allan; Maurice
O'Castelan (called also Maurice Okerfair); Reginald;
Brennus; and Donald.—(See Sacheverell, *Short Survey of the
Isle of Man*, vol. i., *Manx Society*, p. 66.)

The Isle of Man became involved in the confusion
incident to the claims of the families of Bruce, Baliol, and

other competitors for the Scottish throne; and being left "desolate and oppressed with many miseries," the Manx placed themselves under the protection of Edward the First of England, in 1290.—(See *Rymer's Foedera*, vol. ii., p. 492; see also Sacheverell's *Short Survey*, vol. i., *Manx Society*, note 74, p. 67.) Edward the First made grants of the Island to various parties, the first of whom was John Baliol of Scotland, in 1292. The right of Baliol was opposed by the families of Montacute and Waldeboef, descendants on the female side, from the ancient Norse Kings of Man. Baliol was deposed and thrown into prison by Edward, in 1296; and died in France, in 1304. In 1306, it is most likely that Sir William Montacute (son of Sir Simon Montacute, to whom Aufrica or Affreca de Connaught, the sister of Magnus, last King of Man, had made over her right that same year—see Sacheverell's *Short Survey of the Isle of Man*, p. 68), proceeded to take possession of his ancestral dominions; but in order to meet the expenses to which he had been put in so doing, was obliged to mortgage the revenues of the Isle of Man, to Anthony Bec.—(See *Text*, p. 23.) His rights seem not to have been recognised by Edward the Second, who made grants of the Island to the various parties named by our author. But in 1313, Robert Bruce, King of Scotland, landed at Ramsey, in the Isle of Man, and proceeding to Castletown, after a somewhat lengthened siege, took Rushen Castle; and the power of the Bruce Party was then established on the Isle, and continued for the most part till the conquest of the Isle from the Scotch, by the English, under Sir William Montacute (First Earl of Salisbury, and son of the former Sir William Montacute), in 1343.—(See notes 78 and 79, to Sacheverell's *Short Survey, Manx Society*, vol. i.)

It is evident that our author counts the 74 years of the tenure of the Isle of Man by the Scotch, from 1270 to 1343 inclusive; but during a portion of that period, *viz.*, from 1290 to 1313, the Island was clearly in the hands of the Kings of England (Edward the First and Edward the Second) and their nominees, and was jointly occupied by the English and such of the Scotch as were opposed to the claims of Bruce. After the battle of Bannockburn, many Scottish families who were obnoxious to the Earl of Carrick, then struggling for the Scottish throne, seem to have taken refuge in the Isle of Man; and we are thus enabled to explain Bruce's expedition to the Isle of Man, in 1313, and the obstinate defence of Rushen Castle against him, by Duncan de Ergadia, or Duncan Macdougall (the Dingawi Macdoual of the *Chronicon Manniae*), who was cousin to the Second Red Comyn, muidered by Bruce at Dumfries, in 1306-7.—(See *Genealogical Table of the Ergadia Family, Appendix B.*) Bruce never felt himself safe even after the murder of Comyn, as long as any of that nobleman's kindred remained.

In connection with this tenure of the Isle by the Scots, mentioned by our author, it may be well to examine here more particularly the statement of Sacheverell, as above referred to, respecting its conquest by them, as it seems to explain in some measure the interest acquired by Henry de Beaumont, as narrated by our author, pages 24-28.

The words of Sacheverell (see *Short Survey of the Isle of Man*, vol. i., *Manx Society*, p. 65) are, "Alexander (King of Scotland,—EDIT.) having now reduced all the outisles, sends a numerous army under Alexander of Peasely and John Comyne, who landed at Rannesway, in the year 1270."

It is not easy to determine which of the John Comyns it was who took so active a part in this expedition. On refemng to the Genealogical Table of the Comyn family (see *Appendix D.*), it will be seen that there were in 1270 at least *four* John Comyns, who were of sufficient note and standing to be entrusted with the command of the invading army.

There was then living the *first* Red Comyn, John Lord of

Badenoch, who in 1264, along with John Baliol and Robert Bruce, led troops into England, to assist Henry the Third, against his refractory Barons. He was son of Sir Richard Comyn; and grandson by the first wife, of that Sir William Comyn who became Earl of Buchan, in right of his second wife, Marjorie, only daughter and heiress of Fergus, Earl of Buchan. He is also said by Shaw, in his *History of the Province of Moray*, to have married Marian, a daughter of Alan, Lord of Galloway.—(See *Appendix A.*)

Next, there was John Comyn, son of the *first* Red Comyn. He was called the *Black* Comyn; and married Marjorie, sister of John Baliol, King of Scotland.

Again, there was John, the *second* Red Comyn, son of the Black Comyn, by his wife Marjorie, and who was therefore nephew to King John Baliol. He was that Comyn murdered by Robert Bruce in the Church at Dumfries, in 1306-7, being a competitor with him for the crown of Scotland; and having a prior claim to it both from Hexilda, through his father, and from David, Earl of Huntingdon, through his mother, the sister of King John Baliol.

Lastly, there was at the same time John Comyn, who became Earl of Buchan, succeeding his father, Alexander, Earl of Buchan, in 1288. He was made High Constable of Scotland, and swore fealty to Edward the First, at Norham, in June, 1291. As the holder of a Barony in England (*viz.*, that of Whitwic, in Leicestershire), he was summoned to perform military duty with the army which had been ordered to assemble at Norham, at the end of six weeks after Easter (see *Parliamentary Writs of England*). He it was who (as above observed in note 17), obtained leave from Edward the First to dig for lead in the Calf of Man, to cover eight towers of his Castle at Cruggleton, in Galloway; having succeeded to the Galloway estates in right of his mother, Elizabeth, daughter of Roger de Quincy, Earl of Winchester, and grand-daughter

of Alan, Lord of Galloway (see *Appendix A*). An illegitimate
son of this Alan, was the notorious Mac Dhu Alan, who
married a daughter of Reginald, the usurping King of Man
(the same who made surrender to the Pope, in 1219), bastard
son of Godred the Black, King of Man (see *Chronicon
Manniae*). Through this daughter of Reginald, Thomas Mac
Dhu Alan became brother-in-law of Godred Don, who had
two sons, Harold and Ivar; the latter of whom is particularly
mentioned as the murderer of Reginald (Olaveson), King of
Man, in 1249 (see *Chronicon Manniae*), and the former
seized the Kingdom of Man, in 1250. Sacheverell states from
Manx tradition (see *Short Survey*, p. 54), that the widow of
Magnus, the last Scandinavian King of Man, was secretly in
love with this Ivar; and he leads us to infer that it was on her
account that Ivar led the Manx army, which resisted the
invasion of the Scotch, at the battle of Ronaldsway, in 1270;
in which battle, as before noted, Ivar and 536 of the flower of
the Manx nation fell.

> "L decies X ter, et pente duo cecidere
> Mannica Gens de te, damna futura cave."
>   (*Chronicon Manniae.*)

It was, however, quite as likely that Ivar on that occasion
fought in support of his own pretensions to the throne of
Man, as of any which the widow of Magnus might be
presumed to have entertained; for he was the nearest male
descendant of Godred the Black (see *Appendix C*), and his
grandfather Reginald, though illegitimate, had occupied the
throne of Man and the Isles for 38 years. He may have
thought to strengthen the number of his partisans by uniting
himself with the widow of Magnus; but in reality her claim
to the throne could never stand in competition with that of
Mary, the daughter of Reginald (Olaveson), or with that of
Aufrica (or Affreca) de Connaught, the sister of this
Reginald, and aunt of Mary.

Ivar seems to have been connected with the Comyns of the Buchan line, and also with those of Badenoch, if we dare rest on the authority (above referred to) of Shaw, in his *History of the Province of Moray*, For Helena, the wife of Roger de Quincy, and mother of Elizabeth, who married Alexander Comyn, Earl of Buchan, was daughter of Alan, Lord of Galloway, with whom Ivar's father was connected by his sister, married to Alan's son Thomas; and Shaw also states that the First Red Comyn married Marian, daughter of Alan. The difficulty in the way of receiving Shaw's statement, for which he has not given authority, is that we have positive information of only three *legitimate* daughters of Alan: *viz.*, by his first wife (name unknown), Helena, married to Roger de Quincy; by his second wife (Margaret, daughter of David, Earl of Huntingdon), Christian, married in 1236, to William de Fortibus (son and heir of the Earl of Albemarle), and Devorgille, married in 1233, to John de Baliol, of Barnard Castle. Alan had by his third wife (a daughter of Henry de Lacy), no issue (see Chalmer's *Caledonia*), It is remarkable, however, that Buchanan says, that in 1258 "the Cumins had now great power in Galloway; Mary, the sister of Devorgille, having married John Cumin." His exact words are "Balliolus per matrem totam Gallovidiam regionem amplissimam tenebat; Cuminiam familiam secundum Reges potentissimam affinitate sibi junctam habebat per Johannem Cuminium *cui Maria Dornagillae Soror nupserat*."—(See Buchanan's *Rerum Seoticarum Historia*, lib. viii., p. 134.) Dr. Taylor, of Elgin, is of opinion that the John Comyn here referred to, is the *Black Comyn* who married Marjory, the *daughter* of Devorgille, and sister to John Baliol; and he adds that there is no evidence that Devorgille had a sister Mary. If Buchanan's statement be taken as *literally* correct, that John Comyn had married "Maria *Soror* Dornagillae," the presumption would be that this Maria was the same as Shaw's

Marian; and that she was not only legitimate, but the daughter of Margaret, daughter of David, Earl of Huntingdon. This would have made the claim of her son John, the Black Comyn, to the throne of Scotland, next in order to that of King John Baliol, whose sister he married. Yet it seems strange that if there were such a claim by direct descent from David, Earl of Huntingdon, it should never (as far as I know), have been put forward in behalf of the *Black* Comyn. The claim which he himself put forward, was that derived by his direct descent from Hexilda, the grand-daughter of Donald Bane, King of Scotland.

Of the four John Comyns above mentioned, the two youngest, at the time of the battle of Ronaldsway, 1270, were John Comyn, son of Alexander Comyn Earl of Buchan; and John (the Second Red Comyn), cousin to John de Ergadia, whose mother was the third daughter of the First Red Comyn, and sister to the Black Comyn. Yet, as they both at a very early age acquired military renown, it is not impossible that either of them may have been employed in the Manx Expedition. Dr. Taylor suggests that it may have been very probably the Second Red Comyn who was so employed, for there is evidence that, young as he was, he had before 1270 attained to military honours; since, according to Fordoun, he had been Knighted by Alexander the Third, in 1267, (*Scotichronicon*, vol. ii., p. 108,) "Ubi etiam Johannes filius Johannis Comyn, ab ipso rege Alexandro baltheo precingitur militari." And in the chapter next to that in which this quotation occurs, but under date 1268, Fordoun says "Rex Alexander versus Man exercitum citari fecit, ibidem contra insultus rebellium castramentatus. Tandem inito consilio quosdam de suis cum Galweyensibus illuc transmisit; et exercitus reversus est." That the John Comyn above mentioned as being Knighted, was the *Second* Red Comyn, and not his father, the Black Comyn, is plain from the circumstance that the Black Comyn had been Knighted at a previous date, Fordoun speaking of him as already a Knight, in 1266 (vol. ii., p. 103), "Johannes Comyn et alii *milites*."

Very little is said in history of any military exploits of the Black Comyn. He was one of the six Guardians of Scotland, on the death of Alexander the Third; and as we know, one of the competitors for the throne of Scotland. He died at his Castle of Lochindorb, in Moray, in 1299, leaving his son John, the Second Red Comyn, as competitor for the throne, against Robert Bruce.

John Comyn, Lord of Badenoch, the *First* Red Comyn, was a distinguished soldier and statesman in the reign of Alexander the Third; and as above noted, led troops to assist Henry the Third against his Barons: and if it be the case that he had married a daughter of Alan, Lord of Galloway, his presence at the head of Gallovidians, in the invasion of Man, in 1270, would not be improbable.

With respect to the other John Comyn, the son of the Earl of Buchan, the following circumstances are worthy of note. There is in the possession of the present Sir Alexander Penrose Gordon Cumming, Bart., of Altyre, a brass seal, bearing the Coat of Arms of the Earls of Buchan (the three garbs or wheat sheaves, as seen in the shield of pretence on the Coat of Arms of Henry de Beaumont, in the accompanying plate of Chaloner), and round about it the inscription "S: IONIS: COMIN: FIL: COM: DE: BUCHAN"— (the seal of John Comin, son of the Earl of Buchan). It has over it the label indicating that it was the seal of the eldest son, in his father's lifetime. It was therefore the seal either of John Comyn, son of Alexander Comyn, Earl of Buchan, and uncle to Alice, wife of Henry de Beaumont; or of his son John, who died about 1306. Its date must be, if of the former, between 1243 and 1288, when Alexander died; if of the latter between 1288 and 1306. It is stated in the *Scotichronicon* that though William, Earl of Buchan (the father of Alexander), died in 1231, yet his son Alexander was not designated Earl of Buchan, till 1243. Hence, the presumption is that Alexander did not till 1243, arrive at his majority, unless he was simply kept out of the Earldom on account of his mother, the Countess, who died in 1237-8; so that his son John, even if born when his father was only 21 years of age, must have been a minor till 1264 at least, and could be hardly more than 25 in 1270, and most probably was younger than John, the Second Red Comyn, who was Knighted in 1267. Whatever difficulty may therefore on the score of age attach to the assumption that the *Second* Red Comyn led the Scotch at the battle of Ronaldsway, the same must attach in an equal, if not higher degree, to the hypothesis that John Comyn, son of Alexander, Earl of Buchan, was their leader.

It may still be noted that Alexander Comyn, the father of this John, was employed by Alexander the Third, in settling the affairs of the Isles, in 1282. He was thrice summoned to perform military service by Edward the First of England: once in 1277, against Llewellyn, Prince of Wales; and again in 1282. He may have been employed by Alexander against the Isles, in 1270; and his son John may have taken a share in that part of the expedition which was directed against the Isle of Man.

That the Comyns did acquire a considerable interest in Manx affairs, there can be little doubt. As above observed, it was a nephew of the Black Comyn—Duncan de Ergadia, or Duncan Macdougal, (the Lord Dungawi Macdoual of the *Chronicon Manniae*,)—who defended Rushen Castle so vigorously against Robert Bruce, in 1313. One of the family, Alice de Beaumont, if not *actually* styled such, was *really* Queen of Man. It is certain that the power of the Comyn family culminated just at the time when the Isle of Man passed into the hands of the Scotch. Their fall commenced with that of the family of Baliol, with which they were so closely connected, and was completed at the Battle of Bannockburn, when the fortunes of the Bruces rose upon their ruin.

Having figured in the history of Scotland for nearly two centuries, the Comyns "were then suddenly extinguished by forfeiture, banishment, and proscription. "The Cumins" (says Mr. Riddel, in his *Reply to the misstatements of Dr. Hamilton*) "were certainly the most illustrious of our Scottish families; and their blood at this day circulates through all that is noble, in the Sister Kingdom, including even the numerous and royal descendants of King Henry the Fourth."—(See *Appendix D*) In the *Antiquities of the Shires of Aberdeen and Banff*, printed for the *Spalding Club*, 1847, we read "On the 28th of August, 1296, at Berwick on Tweed, Brice, Abbot of Deir, swore fealty to King Edward the First, of England." About the same time, or between the years 1290 and 1308, the Monastery obtained from John, Earl of Buchan, a grant of the patronage of the Church of Kyn-Edwart. This gift, from the grandson of their founder, was the last which the Brethren of St. Mary were fated to receive from his race and lineage. In the memorable Revolution which placed the Earl of Carrick on the Scottish Throne, the illustrious family of Cumyn was so utterly overthrown, that, says a Chronicle of the age, "of a name which numbered at one time three Earls, and more than thirty belted Knights—De nomine Cumyng erant tres comites Buchanie, Marre et Menteith et simul xxx milites baltheo accincti—there remained no memorial in the land, save the orisons of the Monks of Deir. The new King wasted the heritage of the Cumyns with such cruelty,

> That eftre that weile fyfty yer,
> Men menyt (bewailed) the herschip of Bowchane."

It is not improbable that some of the relics of the fallen family may be traced in the Isle of Man, under the Manx

"Comish," presenting a singular addition to the many forms
in which the name of this family has been spelt. In the Roll
of Battle Abbey, we find it as originally Comin; but various
Charters and public documents afterwards exhibit it as
Comine, Comyn, Comyne, Cumin, Cummin, Cumine,
Cumyn, Cumyne, Cwmyn, Cuming, Cumyng, and
Cumming; to which may be added a further English
corruption of it, by the addition of the letter *s* to most of the
above forms.

Note 57.—"Even to our times."

In the original of Chaloner's description, immediately
after the sentence "even to our times," great confusion is
produced by the transposition to this place of the documents
pertaining to Lord Beaumont; and the omission, in the
proper place, of all mention of Anthony Bec and Piers
Gaveston; as well as the recovery of the Island by the Scots,
under Robert Bruce, and its reconquest by William
Montacute the younger, Earl of Salisbury, in 1343. This was
attempted to be rectified in the addenda to the book, but in
a very clumsy manner. In the re-arrangement of the text, I
have been obliged to omit a few words of Chaloner, in order
to make it consistent with the true chronology. In the
original, Chaloner, after stating that Anthony Bec, Bishop of
Durham and Patriarch of Jerusalem, held the Isle of Man for
seven years, goes on to say "Then "William Montacute, son
of the said William Earl of Salisbury, possessed the same."
So far, *with certain omissions*, he is correct; but in trying to
correct his text in the addenda, he falls into a gross error, for
he says that "William Montacute the younger, (First—EDIT.)
Earl of Salisbury, in the year 1340 (1343—EDIT.) won it from
the Scots, and sold it for a great sum of money to Sir
"William Scroop." It was not, however, the Sir William
Montacute who conquered the Isle in 1343, who sold it to

Lord Scroop; but his son, Sir William Montacute, Second Earl of Salisbury, who succeeded his father in the Kingdom of Man, in the year 1344.

In my notes to the first volume of the *Manx Society* (Sacheverell's *Short Survey of the Isle of Man*), an attempt is made to reconcile Camden, Chaloner, and Sacheverell, with each other and with the facts of history which are elicited by the comparison of the ancient documents, puhlished in vol. vii. of the *Manx Society*.

Note 58.—"Mary, the daughter of Reginald, the last King of Man, of that name."

There is a mistake here, copied by many writers, and leading to considerable confusion in this portion of Manx history. This "Mary, married to the Earl of Strathem," was not the *daughter*, but the *widow* of Reginald Olaveson; as appears hy the following passage in Fordoun, "Rex Manniae mortuus est; cujus *relictam* Comes Malisius de Strathern postea duxit, scilicet filiam Eugenii de Ergadia."—(*Scotichronicon*, vol. ii., p. 109.) In Rymer's *Faedera*, vol. i., part 2, p. 773 (printed in vol. vii., *Manx Society*, p. 116), she is styled "Nobilis mulier Maria regina de Man, et Comitissa de Strathern;" her name being given amongst those who did homage to Edward the First, of England, in 1292, in the Church of the Predicant Brethren, at Perth. She was again a widow in 1296; for we read under that date "Maria que *fuit* uxor Malisii Comitis de Strathern;" and as such she received from Edward the First a precept addressed to the Sheriff of Perth, for the restoration of the estates which had belonged to her late husband.—(*Rot. Scot.*, vol. i., p. 26.) She had a daughter by Reginald: *viz.*, Mary, married to John de Waldeboef, from whom descended a son William, and grandson John; the last of whom prosecuted his claim to the Crown of Man, derived from her, and was ordered to be heard in the King's Bench, 33 Edward the First.—(See *Rot. Parl.*, A.D. 1306 and *Appendix C.*)

She had also by the Earl of Strathern a son (Malise), who became Earl of Strathern, and is mentioned as a prisoner in England, in 1306 and 1310 (*Rymer*, vol. i., part 2, p. 1003; and *Rot. Scot.*, vol. i., p. 94); and it is most probably *his* wife who is the Countess of Strathern mentioned as being implicated in the conspiracy against Robert the First of Scotland, in 1320. For it seems very improbable that Mary (the Dowager Countess), who was the widow of Reginald and a mother in 1249, should take part in a conspiracy in 1320, when she must have been 90 years of age at least, if she were living.

The generally received opinion is that Mary, the wife of Reginald Olaveson, was the daughter, not of *Ewen*, or Eugene de Ergadia (as stated by Fordoun), but of *Alexander* de Ergadia, and therefore, that she was sister of John de Ergadia; and I so expressed it in 1859, in my notes to vol. i., *Manx Society* (Sacheverell's *Short Survey*, p. 160), on an authority which was furnished to me, and said to be from the *Ragman Roll* (but which I have since then found to have been incorrectly given), tracing through this lady the connection of the Comyns and Beaumonts with the Isle of Man. The same opinion is expressed by Dr. Oliver, in vol. iv., *Manx Society*, note to p. 213, "Reginald married Mary, daughter of *Alexander* de Ergadia, Lord of Lorn." I must now, for myself, retract that opinion; believing Fordoun to be correct in his speaking of Mary as "filiam *Eugenii* de Ergadia." Dr. Taylor, of Elgin, has kindly pointed out to me a considerable difficulty to be urged against the hypothesis that she was the daughter of *Alexander* de Ergadia. He says "if she were the daughter of Alexander de Ergadia, he must have been nearly 100 years old in 1301, when he retired to England, after his defeat by Bruce. The date of his *death* there, is not mentioned.—(*Fordoun*, vol. ii., p. 242.) Admitting that Mary was only 18 years of age when she became the widow of

Reginald, King of Man, in 1249, her father, if 21 years old at the time of her birth, must in that case have been born in 1211." It is right, however, to state, that Skene says, in opposition to Fordoun, that it was *John* de Ergadia who retired to England, in 1308. He says (vol. ii., p. 110), "Alaster of Lorn, hopeless of successfully continuing his opposition, submitted to the victorious King; while his son John, who could not expect to be admitted to any terms, fled to England." Still, this would shew, that Alaster was living in 1308; and the same difficulty would arise. A far greater difficulty would arise, if we accept the statement of Sir Walter Scott and Skene, followed by Train and other writers, that Alexander de Ergadia "married the third daughter of John, the Red Comyn, slain by Bruce."—(See *Lord of the Isles*, note to First Canto, p. 24.) For the Red Comyn was slain by Bruce, in 1306-7; and if Mary, the wife of Reginald, were the daughter of *Alexander* de Ergadia, she would consequently be the grand-daughter of this Second Red Comyn; and as she had a daughter Mary, in 1249, we should arrive at the conclusion, that a man, active enough to be a competitor with Robert Bruce, for the throne of Scotland, in 1306, was a great-grandfather 67 years before that time. Further, John de Waldeboef, the great-grandson of Reginald and Mary, was old enough in 1304, to be prosecuting his claim to the Throne of Man; and if the John Comyn, slain by Bruce, were the grandfather of the wife of Reginald, he would have been living and active at the time when his great-great-great-grand-son was of mature age.

Sir Walter Scott contradicts himself, and makes the matter still worse when he says (*History of Scotland*, in Dr. Lardner's *Cabinet Cyclopdedia*, p. 91), "Macdougal, or John of Lorn, married an aunt of the slaughtered Comyn." If John of Lorne's father (Alaster de Ergadia), married a daughter of the murdered Comyn, and he himself (John of Lorn), married

Comyn's aunt, we should have a man marrying his grandfather's aunt; a relationship not contemplated in the table of marriages, within prohibited degrees. John of Lorn was in reality first cousin of the murdered Red Comyn. The same error as to the wife of Alaster de Ergadia, occurs in Harvey's *Life of King Robert Bruce*, wherein John of Lorn is mentioned as the *nephew* of the John Comyn whom Bruce and Kirkpatrick murdered—"McDougal *nephew* to the Cumine slain."

I believe that most of these errors have originated from the fact that Sir Walter Scott, and the other writers who have followed him, were ignorant of, or overlooked the circumstance of there having been two Red Comyns, the father and the son respectively of John, the Black Comyn.— (See *Appendix D*.) It is also plain that Ewen, or Eugene de Ergadia, has been confounded with Alaster de Ergadia; a very distant relative, though living at the same time.—(See *Appendix B*.) Lord Hailes, in the *Annals of Scotland*, vol. ii., p. 8, gives, on the authority of Fordoun and Archdeacon Barbour, the correct statement, that "Alexander of Argyle, Lord of Lorn, had married the aunt of Comyn;" *i.e.*, of the Comyn slain by Bruce. And with this statement it is evident that those lines of Wyntoun most fully agree, though adduced by Sir Walter Scott, in support of *his* view (note to Canto the First, Lord of the Isles).

> "The thryd douchtyr of Red Comyn
> Alysawnder of Argayle syne
> Tuk and weddyt til hys wyf
> And on hyr he gat until hys lyf
> John of Lorn."

The Second Red Comyn, son of John the Black Comyn (Lord of Badenoch, and brother-in-law of John Baliol), is thus seen to have been the first cousin to John of Lorn, who had great possessions in the Isle of Man; claiming an interest therein probably as a descendant of Somerled, Thane of Argyle.—(See *Appendix B.*) John of Lorn thoroughly espoused his cousin's cause against Bruce; as we read in *The Brus*, edited by Cosmo Innes, p. 145:—

> "This Johne of Lorne hatit the King (Robert Bruce)
> For Schire Johne Cumyn his emis' sak."

He may have retired to his estates in the Isle of Man, when his father, Alexander, retired to England, in 1308; but if so, he was driven out in 1313, when Robert Bruce took the Island, with the Castle of Rushen, which was defended by John of Lorn's brother, Duncan (Dungawi Macdoual); nor did he regain possession of his property there till 1340.

Note 59.—"Henry, Lord Beaumont."

Henry de Beaumont was son of Lewis de Brenne, by Agnes (his wife). Viscountess de Beaumont and Mayne. This Lewis de Brenne was according to some authorities the son of Charles, Earl of Anjou (a younger son of Lewis the Eighth, King of France); according to others, the second son of John de Brenne, the last King of Jerusalem.—(See Burke's *Extinct Peerage*.)

He is said to have come into England in the suite of Queen Eleanor. It appears (see *Edward the First in the North of Scotland*, by Dr. Taylor, p. 262) from the testimony of the Minstrel Blind Harry, (*The Wallace*, edited by Dr. Jamieson, p. 338-9,) that he was in Scotland in 1297; and again (according to Dugdale), with Edward the First, in 1303, when he obtained a precept to the collectors of fifteenths in Yorkshire, for 200 marks, for his support during the war. He had a residence at Bundarg Castle, in Buchan, from which he fled, on the first expedition of William Wallace and his friends into Buchan."

> "Out of Murray in Bowchane land com thai
>   To sek Bewmond, be he past away.
>   Than thir gud men to Wallace passyt rycht."

But

> "Lord' Beaumont tuk the sey at Buchan ness."

Probably one great object in his joining in the expedition of 1303, was the recovery of his estates, and more especially of the lands of Philorth, which he had either seized or obtained on the defection of the Lord of that Barony.—(See *Edward the First in Scotland*, p. 262.)

It is stated by Buchanan (*History of Scotland*, book ix., chap. 16), that Henry de Beaumont married a daughter of Sir John Mowbray. There is, however, no doubt that his wife was a Comyn; the eldest daughter either (as stated by our author and almost certainly) of Alexander Comyn, the second son of Alexander the Second Earl of Buchan; or of his brother, John Comyn, the Third Earl of that family. It is certain that he obtained the Comyn estates, in Leicestershire; and he is the direct ancestor of the Beaumonts of Cole Orton, in that county. He was never acknowledged in Scotland, as Earl of Buchan; nor is there evidence to prove that he obtained his wife's moiety of the Scottish estates; *viz.*, the lands of Cairnbulg, and the other extensive domains of the family, which were confiscated to the crown by Robert the First; though John, son of the Earl of Ross, who had married Margaret Comyn, Alice Beaumont's sister, obtained from Robert by charter, referred to below (*Note* 61), a grant of the half of the territories of the proscribed Earl; and having, as it is said, no family, disposed of them again by charter, in 1316, dated at Inverness, to his elder brother, the Earl of Ross, and failing him, to Hugh, his second son, and after him, to Walter Leslie, who had married the eldest daughter of the Earl of Ross. They were severally designated of Philorth, until the year 1375, when that Barony, including Cairnbulg, came into the hands of Sir Alexander Fraser, of Cowie, by his marriage with the youngest daughter and co-heiress of the Earl, and sister of Euphemia, Countess of Ross.—(See *Buchan*, by John B. Pratt, p. 142.) Henry de Beaumont became a favourite of Edward the Second; and in the first year of that monarch, had a grant in fee of the Manors of Folkynham, Edenham, and Barton-upon-Humber, and of all the Knight's fees belonging to Gilbert de Gant, which Laura de Gant, his widow, held in dower. He was summoned to parliament as a Baron, in 1309.—(Burke's *Extinct Peerage*.) He was also constituted Governor of Roxburgh Castle; aad deputed with Humfrey de Bohun, Earl of Hereford, and Robert de Clifford, to guard the Marches. About this time also, he married Alice Comyn; and in the 6th year of Edward the Second, doing homage, had livery of her lands. On the disgrace of Piers Gaveston, he obtained frt)m Edward the Second a grant of the Isle of Man for life, as seen in the first of the documents pertaining to him.—(Printed also in vol. vii. of the *Manx Society*; Dr. Oliver's *Monumenta*, vol. ii., p. 141, from the *Rot. Orig. in Curia Scaccarii*, 1 Edward the Second, A.D. 1308.) In 1310, Edward the Second resumed possession of the Isle of Man, out of Beaumont's hands, and granted it to Anthony de Bec, Bishop of Durham (see vol. vii., *Manx Society*, p. 149); but on the death of that prelate, in 1311, Beaumont appears again as holding the Island in the name of the King, and collecting the revenue thence, as we have a writ (5 Edward the Second, A.D. 1312), addressed to Gilbert Mac Gaskill, Keeper of the Isle of Man, in which he is commanded to deliver to Gilbert de Bromley, all the money which he may receive from Henry de Beaumont, or his Lieutenant in the Island ("de dilecto et fideli nostro Henrico de Bello Monte vel ejus locum tenente in terra predicta."—*Manx Society*, vol vii., p. 154.) But in the same year, Beaumont again obtained a re-grant of the Island for life.—(See *Rot. Orig. in Curia Scaccarii*, 6 Edward the Second, *Manx Society*, vol. vii., p. 158.) It would appear from the second document in Chaloner (Rotuli Parliamentorom, 5 Edward the Second, "Aussint pur ceo," &c.), that the King repented of the large gifts he had bestowed upon Beaumont, mainly through the intrigues of the Lady de Vescy, Beaumont's sister, for he complains that Henry de Beaumont had taken from him "au damage et deshonor du Roi," the Kingdom of Man and other lands, rents, franchises, and bailliwicks, and procured from the donor both other lands and tenements, franchises, and bailliwicks." Beaumont was therefore dismissed from the King's person, and his property taken into the hands of the King until restitution should be made of the King's revenues, which Beaumont had appropriated to himself. The Lady de Vescy, Henry Beaumont's sister, was also banished to her family, and forbidden to return to St. James's Court to live.

Whether Henry de Beaumont was subsequently recognised as Lord of Man, does not appear; but he was plainly not in *possession* of it, as Robert Bruce landed at Ramsey, in 1313, besieged and took Rushen Castle, and then gave a charter to Thomas Randolph, Earl of Moray, to hold the Isle of Man under him (see vol. vii., *Manx Society*, p. 162, and vol. ix., p. 13); and it is to be observed that Henry de Beaumont's name is not given as Lord of Man in the last of the three documents in Chaloner (see also Rymer's *Faedera*, 16 Edward the Second, A.D. 1323), ordering his commitment to prison on account of disobedience to the King.

In the 10th year of Edward the Second, Lord Beaumont, being then the King's Lieutenant in the north, accompanying thither two Cardinals who had come from Rome, partly to reconcile the King to the Earl of Lancaster, and partly to enthronize his Lordship's brother, Lewis de Beaumont, in the Bishopric of Durham, was attacked near

Darlington by a band of robbers, headed by Gilbert de Middleton, and despoiled of all his treasures, horses, and everything else of value. Lord Beaumont was conveyed to the Castle of Mitford, and his brother, the Bishop, to the Castle of Durham, as prisoners, remaining there till ransomed.—(See Burke's *Extinct Peerage*.) Notwithstanding his quarrel with the King, in 1323, he was shortly afterwards restored to the King's favour; and two years subsequently, was constituted one of the plenipotentiaries to treat of peace with France; and also in 1326, was nominated guardian to David de Strathbolgi (son and heir of David de Strathbolgi, Earl of Athol, deceased; and grandson of the Second Red Comyn), in consideration of the sum of one thousand pounds.—(See *Appendix D.*)

He shortly after this deserted entirely the cause of the King, and siding with the Queen Consort Isabella, was the very person to deliver him up to his enemies, upon his abortive attempt to flee beyond the seas. The King was committed a close prisoner to Berkeley Castle; and there, as is well known, barbarously murdered. As the reward of his treachery, Lord Beaumont received a grant of the Manor of Loughborough, part of the possessions of Hugh le Despenser, the attainted Earl of Winchester; and was summoned to Parliament on the 22nd January, 1334 (7th Edward the Third), as Earl of Buchan.

During the reign of Edward the Third, he had many high and confidential employments, and took a prominent part in the affairs of Scotland, being at one time sent as Constable of the King's Army, into that country.

On the decease of his sister, the Lady Isabella (widow of John de Vescy, of Alnwick, in Northumberland), without issue, he obtained her large possessions in the County of Lincoln, and thus became one of the most wealthy nobles in the kingdom. He died in 1340, leaving several children, of whom John, Second Baron Beaumont, was summoned to Parliament 25th Feb., 1342, but was never entitled Earl of Buchan; and Elizabeth, married to Nicholas de Audley, son and heir of James, Lord Audley, of Heley.—(Burke's *Extinct Peerage.*) He had also other daughters, the fifth of whom, Isabella, married Henry Plantagenet, Duke of Lancaster (see *Appendix D.*), and he thus.became a progenitor of King Henry the Fourth.

There were descended from Lord Henry de Beaumont, six Barons of the same name, the last of whom, William de Beaumont, Second Viscount de Beaumont, and Seventh Baron, dying without issue, in 1507, the Viscountcy expired, and the Barony of Beaumont fell into abeyance, according to the decision upon the claims of Thomas Stapleton, Esq., in 1798. Sir George Howland Willoughby Beaumont, Bart., of Cole Orton, Leicestershire, is descended from Sir Thomas Beaumont, Kt, Lord of Basquerville, in Normandy (second son of John de Beaumont, the Sixth Baron, Knight of the Garter), who was created First Viscount Beaumont, in 1409. This Sir Thomas Beaumont, married Philippa, daughter and heiress of Thomas Maureward, Esq., of Cole Orton; he died in 1457, leaving two sons,—Sir John Beaumont, Knight, of Cole Orton, slain at Towton, in 1461 (the ancestor of Sir G. H. W. Beaumont); and Thomas Beaumont, Esq. (the ancestor of the Beaumonts of Barrow-upon-Trent).

Respecting the origin of the name of the territory from which the Earls of Buchan derived their title, considerable difference of opinion has existed. The name is variously spelt Buchan, Buquhan, and Boghan, and is plainly of Celtic origin. Keith says, it "was so called because abounding of old in pasture, paying its rent in cattle, for the word in Irish signifies cow-tribute." Others have suggested a connection with the Manx. *Boc-awen* or *Water-cow*, and with the *Buccaneers* who levied black mail in cattle; but the most probable derivation is that suggested by the situation of the territory on a promontory of Scotland, well known under the present name of Buchan Ness; *Bouchuan* signifying the land *in the bend of the ocean*. This country, afterwards abounding in corn fields, was well represented in Heraldry by sheaves; the arms of the Earls of Buchan and their descendants being "Azure, three garbs Or." They are, however, properly borne by the Comyns and their descendants, and some have fancifully regarded the three garbs or bundles, as representing the herb Cumin. One branch of the Comyns bearing these arms, acquired the title of Earls of Buchan by marriage; William, son of Richard de Comyn, having married for his second wife Marjorie, daughter of Fergus, Earl of Buchan, about 1220.—(See *Appendix D.*) The same arms have been borne by subsequent Earls of Buchan, of various families; and as a shield of pretence on the coats of arms of those connected with the Comyns by marriage, as is seen in the coat of arms of Henry de Beaumont, as given in the plate of Chaloner, and of the De Bohuns, Earls of Chester, and also of the Talbots, Earls of Shrewsbury. Richard, Lord Talbot, married Elizabeth, daughter of the Second Red Comyn, murdered by Bruce. His great-grandson John, was created Earl of Shrewsbury in 1422. It is stated in the *Antiquities of the Shires of Aberdeen and Banff*, edited by the *Spalding Club*, vol. iv., p. 174, that the descendants of this Earl "long remembered the Lordship of Comyn of Badenoch among their titles, and still carry the arms of that great family." After the Comyns and Henry de Beaumont, we find as Earls of Buchan, first, John Stuart, son of Robert, Duke of Albany, who was created Earl of Buchan, and Constable of France. He was slain at the battle of Vernuil, and George Seton, of Seton (ancestor to the Earls of Winton), having married his only daughter Jane, that family continue to carry the arms of Buchan as a coat of pretence, though the Earldom itself was denied to them. In 1457, James the Second of Scotland, created James, second son of John Stuart, the Black Knight of Lorn, and of his wife, Queen Jane (widow to James the First of Scotland), Earl of Buchan; John, the Master of Buchan, was slain at Pinkie, 1547, leaving one daughter. Christian.

Robert Douglas, son of William Douglas, of Lochleven, became Earl of Buchan, having married the said Christian.

Lastly, James Erskine, eldest son of John, Duke of Mar, having married Mary Douglas, also thus became Earl of Buchan.—(See *View of Aberdeen*, in Pratt's Buchan, pp. 91-92.)

Note 60.—"Charta Edwardi II."

I have arranged these three documents pertaining to Henry de Beaumont, chronologically. In Chaloner's original text, they are not so arranged. After the "Charta Edward II.," the date of which is 1 Edward the Second (A.D. 1308), he introduces the document "De Henrico de Bello Monte propter inobedientiam," the date of which is 16 Edward the Second (A.D. 1323), and then brings in last the extract from the *Patent Rolls*, 5 Edward the Second (A.D. 1312), "Aussint pur ceo q'." I have also given the more correct reading of this last Norman-French document, from the copy of it given in vol vii. of the *Manx Society*; in the original edition of Chaloner, it is full of misprints. These three documents, with others belonging to the same period, and referring to Henry de Beaumont, printed in the same volume, assist us materially in fixing the dates of the events in Manx History, at the beginning of the 14th century, though still not without hesitation. In 1305 (34 Edward the First), John de Waldeboef petitioned Edward the First for his rights in the Isle of Man, and was ordered to be heard in the King's Bench (*Rotuli Parliamentorum*); and in the same year, Aufrica de Connaught,

sister of Magnus, last King of Man, made over her right to
her husband. Sir Simon de Montacute, whose son, Sir
William, there is reason to believe in or about the same year,
obtained the Island, and to pay the expenses to which he had
been put, in prosecuting his rights, mortgaged its revenues
to Anthony Bec, Bishop of Durham. On the 28th June, 1307,
Edward the First, at Caldecote, issued a "Scire facias" to
Anthony Bec, to shew cause why he should not surrender the
Island into his hands. The year following, King Edward the
Second (in the first year of his reign) granted (as stated in the
text) the Island to his favorite. Piers de Gaveston, whom he
had made Earl of Cornwall; and then, upon his execution, to
Henry de Beaumont (according to the first of the three
documents in the text), with Gilbert de Mc Gaskill, as his
Lieutenant. In the 3rd year of his reign, Edward the Second
resumed to himself the Island, from the hands of Henry de
Beaumont (*Rot Originalium in Curia Scaccarii*, vol. vii., *Manx
Society*, p. 143), and then granted it *for life* to Anthony Bec,
with Gilbert de Mc Gaskill as his Senescal. (See *Rotuli
Scotiae*, 4 Edward the Second, vol. vii., *Manx Society*, p. 149,
where, in 1311, "Gilbert Makasky" is spoken of as "Senescal
of the venerable Anthony, Patriarch of Jerusalem and Bishop
of Durham"). Anthony Bec died March 3rd of that year; and
in the year following (5 Edward the Second), as appears by
the *Rot. Orig. in curia Scaccarii*, vol. vii., *Manx Society*, p. 158,
the King again granted the Isle of Man to Henry de Beaumont to hold "for the term of his life, freely and peaceably."
But he was the same year a second time deprived of it, and it
was taken into the hands of the King of England "to hold so
long as that the King shall have received of the issues of those
lands, the value of all the worth the said Henry has taken
from the lands, and received contrary to the said decree."—
(*Rotuli Parliamentorum*, 6 Edward the Second, A.D. 1312,
which is the second of the documents pertaining to Henry

de Beaumont, in the text.) In 1313, Robert Bruce took the
Isle of Man, and gave it by charter to Randolph, Earl of
Moray; but the possession of it seems to have been still
disputed, as in the *Rot. Patent. et Claus. Cancellariae
Hiberniae*, 10 Edward the Second, A.D. 1317, we find a letter
of protection to John, Bishop of Sodor, to visit the Island; and
also instructions from the King, to his beloved and faithful
John de Atay, *keeper of his land* of Man, to whose custody the
King committed the Island, on 6th July, 10 Edward the
Second. The King had also given permission, on the 5th of
May, of the same year to the Abbot of St. Ives, in Ulster, to
go to the Isle of Man, to visit the Abbey of Rushen.—(See vol
vii., *Manx Society*, pp. 168-9-10-11.) It is also evident that the
occupation of the Island by the Scotch, after its conquest by
Bruce, could have been by no means in force or effectual; for
in 1316, according to the *Chronicon Manniae*, Richard de
Mandeville and his brothers, with a band of Irish, taking
advantage of the distractions on the Island, landed at
Ronaldsway, beat the Manx in an engagement at Wardfell
(South Barrule), and roaming over the Island for a month,
and plundering it with the Abbey of Rushen, returned at their
leisure to their ships, laden with booty.

This Richard de Mandeville appears to have been so well
satisfied with this exploit, that he repeated it in 1328; for we
read again, in the *Rot. Pat. et claus. Cancellariae Hiberniae*,
2. Edward the Second (see vol. vii., *Manx Society*, p. 178), that
Richard de Mandeville with a multitude of Scotch felons, had
entered the Island for the purpose of conquering it. The
Scotch appear then to have held their ground for a time, since
in 1329, Martoline, the Almoner to Murray, Regent of
Scotland, was sent to take care of morals and religion in the
Island. But in 1333, Edward the Second directed William
Taylor, of Carlisle, and others, to seize the Island in his hands,
and to safely keep the same.—(See *Manx Society*, vol. vii., p.

180); and on the 8th of June, of the same year, the King committed it to his beloved and faithful William de Montacute, to hold unto the Feast of St. Michael, next ensuing; and still further, on the 9th of August, "remitted and released, and for himself and his heirs quitted claim to the said Sir William Montacute, of all his rights and claim which he had, or in any manner could have to the Island of Man."— (See Rymer's *Faedera*, vol. v., p. 558.) Notwithstanding in 1334, Edward Baliol presenting himself to Edward the Third, swore fealty to him for Scotland and the Isles adjacent, and thus got possession of the Isle of Man. On the expulsion from Scotland of Edward Baliol, who had been intruded by Edward the Third upon the throne, in the place of David the Second, the Isle of Man again fell into the power of the Bruce family, and the inhabitants were obliged to purchase peace from them in 1342, by a fine of 800 marks, obtaining the consent thereto of Sir William Montacute (who had been created Earl of Salisbury, in 1337), and also of King Edward the Third himself.—(*Rot. Scotiae*, 16 Edward the Third.) In 1343, the King furnishing the Earl of Salisbury with men and shipping to prosecute his right, he was successful in gaining possession of his ancestral throne, and was crowned King of Man. He died, however, the following year, being succeeded by his son William, second Earl of Salisbury, who had to keep up a constant struggle against the Scotch during a great part of his reign of 49 years. In his old age, having unfortunately slain his son in a tournament at Windsor, he sold his rights to the crown, in 1393, to Sir William Scrope, Chamberlain to Richard the Second, and who was created Earl of Wiltshire, in 1397.

Note 61.—"Henrico de Bello Monte."

The statement made on the shield of Henry de Beaumont, in the accompanying plate of Chaloner, that

Alice Beaumont, the wife of Henry de Beaumont, was "daughter and coheiress of Alexander Comin, Earl of Buquhan," appears to be perfectly correct, though other genealogies of that lady have been brought forward; and there are difficulties in determining her father, Alexander, ever to have been Earl of Buchan.

The most important authority, in support of Chaloner's statement, is that of Wyntoun, in his *Chronicle*, book 8, chap. 6, vol. ii., p. 54.

> "This Alysawndyre eftir that
> Of [his] Spows twa fayre Dowchtris git;
> Henry de Bowmont the eldest
> Weddyt, and neist her the yhowngast
> Schyre John de Ros tuk til his wyf,
> And furth was hyr swa led hys lyf.
> Bot John that was the elder Brodyr,
> Erle of Buchan before the tother," &c.

The accurate antiquary Macpherson, in the notes to his edition of *Wyntoun*, vol. ii., p. 404, on the above passage, says that:

"He" (Alexander) "was as *certainly* Earl of Buchan, as he was father of the wives of Beaumont and Ross; as appears (1st,) by the evidence of Wyntoun, line 296. (2nd,) by a charter of Robert the First to John Ross, son of the Earl of Ross and Margaret Cumin, daughter of the Earl of Buchan.* (3rd,) by the genealogy of the Beaumonts, wherein Henry's wife (Alice), is daughter and coheiress of Alexander Comyn, Earl of Buchan, in Scotland, son of Alexander Comyn, Earl of Buchan [here follows a quotation from Burton's *Description of Leicestershire*]. For this, no authority is given but his agreement with Wyntoun, whose work he surely never saw; and with King Robert's charter, proves that he wrote from authentic records. (4th,) from a corrupted paragraph of Fordoun, wherein, though he is confounded with his father Alexander, and his brother John, he is made the father of Beaumont's wife."

The great difficulties (which, however, are capable of explanation) in the way of receiving Wyntoun's, and therefore Mc Pherson's and Chaloner's statement, are the following:—

Dugdale states (see *Peerage*, p. 60) that Alice de Beaumont was one of the cousins and heirs of John, Earl of Buchan, Constable of Scotland; according to Wyntoun, she was niece to that Earl of Buchan.

Again, Alexander, the *younger* brother of John, must be presumed to have died *first*, from considerations of the following writ, 28th April, 1313, 6 Edward the Second, which also at first sight seems to make Alice de Beaumont the *grand-daughter* of John, Earl of Buchan.

———————————————————————

* In a roll of missing charters by Robert the First, is "Charta Joannis Ross sonne to the Earl of Ross, in tocher with Margaret Cumyng, doghter to the Earle of Buchan, the half of Buchan's haill lands within Scotland."—(*Buchan*, by the Rev. John B. Pratt, M.A.; Appendix, p. 383.)

Ahhreviatio Hotulorum Origiinalium, vol, i., p. 198.

EDW. II} Rex Rogero de Wellesworth esc' Trent' sal'tm. Sciatis quod cum nuper post mortem Johannis Comyn Comitis de Boghan defuncti, omnes terras &c. capi mandaverimus in manum nostram et per inquisicionem &c. accepimus quod predictus Johannes magistrum Wilhelmum Comyn fratrem suum, de duabus partibus Manerii de Shepesved, Villam de Merkynfeld, Whitenton, Bochardeston et Newton, medietatem ville de Rocheby, ville de Whitewick cum parco de Bredon et omnibus dominicis manerii de Whitewick cum pertinentibus preter situm ejusdem manerii, que prefatus Comes tenuit de nobis in capite, per cartam suam feof- faverat ante mortem ejusdem Johannis propter quod cepimus homagium ipsius Wilhelmi &c., tendenda de nobis et heredibus nostris, juxta tenorem litterarum nostrarum patencium, quas ei fieri fecimus de pardonacione transgressionis quam fecit adquirendo sibi terras et tenentia illa sine licencia nostra, dictusque Wilhelmus advertens se postmodum dictas inquisiciones contra justiciam et secutum fuisse, et in presencia nostra personaliter constitutus, recognoverit se nullum jus habere in terris et tenementis predictis, et ea in manus nostras reddiderit tanquam jus et hereditatem Alicie quam Henricus de Bello Monte duxit in uxorem, et Margarite sororis ejusdem Alicie, neptem et heredem predicti Johannis, cepimus homagium ipsius Henrici de propria parte, ipsos Henricum et Aliciam quam pene etatis reputam licet etatem suam non probaverit ut est moris, &c.—(*Rot.* 14.)

The Whitwick here mentioned, is also noticed in another writ, bearing out the inscription on the shield in Chaloner:— "Henry de Beaumont, Lord of Man, and Lord of Whitwick, in Leicester, in right of his wife, &c."

Abbreviatio Placitorum, p. 230.

MICHAELIS ANNO VICESSIMO ET INCIPIENTE VICESSIMO PRIMO ED. I. LEIC. } "Abbas de Gerewedon implicitat Johannem Comyn dominum de Whytewyke et Shepesvede, et viii alios pro capcione, implicace et interfecice centum porcorum sucrum in foresta de Chamewoode, &c."

Now, I would observe, that though in the first of these writs, the word nept' (neptem) would generally be rendered *grand-daughter*; and thus Alice de Beaumont would appear to have been not the *niece*, according to Wyntoun, but the *grand-daughter* of John Comyn, Earl of Buchan; yet we have a classical authority (though of late date), for rendering neptem "niece," and as there is no other *single* word in Latin for niece, we can well understand the legal scribe of the writ using the word *neptem*. Crawford, in his *Lives and Characters of the Officers of the State in Scotland*, says that "Margaret was the *daughter of the Earl of Buchan*."

Alexander the Second, Earl of Buchan (of the Comyn family), had three sons—John, Alexander, and William; the last of whom became Provost of the Canonry of St. Andrews, and Rector of the Church of St. Mary. John succeeded his father as Third Earl of Buchan, in 1288. He married Isabel Macduff, daughter of Duncan, Earl of Fyffe. The honour of placing the crown upon the head of the Scottish Sovereigns at their coronation, belonged of hereditary right to the family of Macduff; and when Robert Bruce was crowned at Scone, in 1306-7, March 27th, this lady (her brother, as appears by the Norman-French document below, being a prisoner in England, and her son (John?) absent at the Manor of Whitwick, in Leicestershire), herself heroically exercised the right, and placed a circlet of gold wire (the Scottish crown having been carried away by Edward the First) upon the head of Robert Bruce. For this she afterwards suffered severely when she fell into the hands of Edward the First, being shut up for six years in the *kage* or keep, at Berwick Castle. Her husband, in every respect, appears to have retired into private life in England, residing at his Manor of Whitwick, in Leicestershire, where it is probable that he died about 1313. He was certainly dead by April 28th, 1313.

The great difficulty is to determine what family he had; and how his brother Alexander, who died before him, became Earl of Buchan. There is no doubt but that he had a son; and it is probable that he had at least two daughters.

The following documents seem to bear upon the subject:—

(1st,) In the *Scala Chronica*, p. 130, we read, referring to Robert Bruce, "Le dit Robert si fest coroner en rois Descoce a Scone en la feste del Annunciacioun notre Dame, de la

Countesse de Boghan, pur absence de Count *soun fitz*, qui adonges demura en Engleterre a son maner de Vituik ioust Laycestre, a qui l'office del encourounment des roys Descoce apartenoit heritablement, abscent le Count de Fiffe qui al hour estoit en garde le roi en Engleterre." This proves that John Comyn, Third Earl of Buchan, had a son, though his name is not given. It was probably John, who *may* have been married, and had daughters Alice and Margaret, Beaumont and Ross respectively; but of this we have no evidence whatever.

The next document is a charter of William de Lindesay, published by the *Spalding Club*, in the *Antiquities of the Shires of Aberdeen and Banff*, vol. iv., p. 4, and said to be (though I think incorrectly), of the date circa 1310. By it William de Lindesay conveys a grant to the Abbey of Deir, "pro salute mee et antecessorum meorum et successorum, et pro salute *Margarite Comitisse de Bucquhan* quondam sponse mee, et Alicie de Lindesay prioris sponse mee," &c. This lady (Margaret, Countess of Buchan), must surely have been either the daughter of John, Third Earl of Buchan, or the relict of his son, or just possibly the daughter of that son; and if the relict, and the presumed date of the charter be correct, then it would follow that this son must have been dead some time prior to 1310.

If the following charter refer to this lady (though I believe it does not), we should then be able to determine not only that John, Third Earl of Buchan, had a son, but that *certainly* his name was John; and that he, too, had a son, named Admor or Aymer. It is recorded in *Abbreviatio Rotulorum Originalium*, vol. i., p. 209.

NOTTINGH' NORTH' ED. II. } Rex &c, salutem. Sciatis quod cum nos nuper considerantes qualiter bone memorie Johannes Comyn filius Johannis Comyn dudum defuncti erga dominum Edwardum nuper Regem Anglie patrem nostrum, et postmodum erga nos fideliter se gesserit &c. quod terre et tenentia in partibus Scocie per Scotos inimicos et rebelles nostros vastantur et destruuntur, volentesque eundem Johannem eo pretextu prospicere gratiose, concessimus ei maneria subscripta viz.:—Manerium de Mannesfeld in Comitatu Nottinghamiensi cum soka et firma de Lynebj et cum molendinis de Carbelton in valorem quinquaginta et quatuor librorum et manerium de Harewell, in comitatu Berkhamiensi, in valorem triginta librarum per annum, tenenda in subsidium Expensarum suarum et sustentacionis sue quamdiu nobis placuerit.

Nos eciam volentes Margarite que fuit uxor prefati Johannis qui in obsequio nostro &c, concessimus ei maneria predicta tenenda &c., in subsidium sustentacionis sue et Admori filii eorundem Johannis et Margarite quamdiu nobis placuerit.

It must, however, be observed, that the expression in the above charter "Margarite que *fuit* uxor prefati Johannis," indicates that Margaret was dead at the time of the grant to her husband, John Comyn, so that *she* could not have been the same Margaret who was the second wife of William de Lindesay.

I am therefore inclined to believe that Margaret de Lindesay was a daughter of John Comyn, Third Earl of Buchan, and that her brother was dead at the time of her marriage with William de Lindesay; and though, if the assumed date of the charter to the Abbey of Deir be correct, her mother Isabel, daughter of Duncan, Earl of Fyffe, was then alive, she might then be termed Countess of Buchan, since her mother, confined for presumed rebellion, in the castle at Berwick, might be considered as having forfeited all her titles, and was not released till April 28th, 1313, when she was given into custody of her nephew-in-law, Henry de Beaumont, her husband being dead.

In the genealogical table (*Appendix D.*) I have inserted
another daughter *Violet*, married to William Urquhart, of
Cromarty, styled De Monte Alto. For it is said that this
William Urquhart married secondly Violet, daughter of John
Comyn, Earl of Buchan and Lord of Strathbolgie (for a time
on the forfeiture of David, Eleventh Earl of Athol); and that
Hugh, Earl of Ross, whose daughter had been William
Urquhart's first wife, was so incensed at his marrying a
Comyn, that he demanded his forfeiture. But William
Urquhart always proving faithful to Robert Bruce, was
restored to his estates, by David the Second.

The question may arise here who was that Margaret
Comyn mentioned as his great-grandmother, by the Earl of
Dunbar and March, in a letter which he wrote to King Henry
the Fourth of England, in 1400? wherein he says "Gif Dame
Alice de Beaumont was your grand-dame (she was great-
grandmother—see *Appendix D.*), dame Marjorie Cumyn was
my grand-dame on to'ther side, so that I am bot of the fierde
degree of kyn to you."—(See Pinkerton's *History*, and
Appendix D.) The inference from the above letter is that this
Marjorie was sister to Alice Beaumont, both being, as
assumed if not proved above, daughters of Alexander
Comyn, Earl of Buchan. But Margaret Ross is always
presumed to have had no family, and this is given as the
reason (though I do not consider it conclusive in those
troubled times), why the "half of the haill lands of Buchan,
within Scotland," were disposed of by her husband, John, son
of the Earl of Ross, to his elder brother, as before remarked
in note 59. It is, however, not improbable that Margaret Boss
may have survived her husband, John de Ross, and then
married the Earl of Dunbar and March, and by him had a
family. Or, the Earl of Dunbar and March, in 1400, in writing
to Henry the Fourth, may have mistaken a generation, for
he was descended from Bridget Comyn, the aunt of the

above Margaret Ross.—(See *Appendix D*.)

To suppose that Marjorie, the great-grandmother of the Earl of Dunbar and March, was a sister of Alice Beaumont, and not the same person as Margaret Ross; and that Margaret Ross was the sister of Violet, and daughter of John Comyn, Earl of Buchan, can hardly be made to agree with the charters I have above referred to, and would be inconsistent with the *statement* of Wyntoun, above quoted, that Margaret Ross was the daughter of Alexander Comyn, and sister of Alice Beaumont.

Again, with reference to the Margaret, the wife of John Comyn, and mother of Aymer Comyn, mentioned in the charter of Edward the Second, above given, out of *Abbreviatio Rotulorum Originalium*, vol. i., p. 209; I believe that she had nothing to do with any of the above Margarets, but that John Comyn, therein named as her husband, and son of John Comyn, "dudum defuncti," was John, the son of the Second Red Comyn, murdered by Robert Bruce. This John Comyn fled to England upon the murder of his father, in 1306-7; and it is stated (in Sir Harris Nicholas's *Historic Peerage of England*, p. 123: new edition, edited by William Courthorpe, Esq.,) that he died in 1325, leaving his two sisters—Joan, wife of David, Earl of Athol, and Elizabeth, wife of Richard, Lord Talbot (from whom are descended the Earls of Shrewsbury)—his co-heirs." In a note on the above passage by the editor, it is added "his son Adomer, or Aymer Comyn, died, vit. pat. A.D. 1316, and by an inquest taken in the same year, his aunts, named in the text, were found to be his heirs." The mother of this John Comyn being a sister of Aymer de Valence, Earl of Pembroke, we can easily understand how her son came to get the christian name of Aymer, which is otherwise entirely foreign to the Comyn family.

Taking all the above-mentioned circumstances into consideration, I think it most probable that John Comyn,

Third Earl of Buchan, on the death of his son, and of his daughter, Margaret de Lindesay (his daughter Violet being married to William Urquhart, a favorer of Robert Bruce), made over in his own lifetime, his titie of Earl of Buchan to his brother Alexander, the father of Alice Beaumont and her sister Margaret; and thus our author will appear perfectly correct in saying that Henry de Beaumont, Lord of Man, was "Lord of Witwic, in Leicester, in right of his wife, daughter and co-heiress of Alexander Comin, Earl of Buquhan."

How the Comyn family came to be interested in Manx affiirs, we may learn from the following considerations, as shewn in the notes above, and the *Appendices*.

John, the Black Comyn, was descended through his mother Marian, daughter of Alan, Lord of Galloway, from Somerled, Thane of Argyle, who conquered Godred the Black, King of Man, at Ramsey, on Jan. 6th, 1156, and placed Dugald, his eldest son (by Affrica, daughter of Olave Kleining, King of Man), on the throne of the Isles. There was a further connection through Marian's illegitimate brother, Thomas Mc Dhu Alan, who married the daughter of Reginald, King of Man.

Alexander Comyn, Earl of Buchan, had a similar connection through his wife, Elizabeth, the daughter of Helena, Countess of Winchester, daughter of Alan, Lord of Galloway.

John Comyn (probably the Second Red Comyn), in conjunction with Alexander Stewart, conquered the Isle of Man for the Scotch, in 1270.

John Comyn, Earl of Buchan, had a grant to open lead mines in the Calf of Man, in 1292.

The mother of John de Ergadia, who had large possessions in the Isle of Man, and whose brother Duncan defended Rushen Castle against Robert Bruce, in 1313, was the daughter of John, the First Red Comyn.

Alice Comyn, wife of Henry de Beaumont, was Queen of Man, in. 1312.

Egidia Comyn, third daughter of Alexander Comyn, Earl of Buchan, married Malise, Earl of Strathern, the son of Mary de Ergadia, who was Queen of Man, in 1249, being then wife of Reginald, King of Man.

Note 62.—"Presenting a cast of faulcons."

This tenure was kept up till 1820, when John, Fourth Duke of Athol, who had been Lord of Man for 45 years, rendered the accustomed service of a cast of falcons, at the coronation of George the Fourth.

Note 63.—"Surmounteth them all."

At the Restoration, the Isle of Man reverted to the Derby family; and Charles, Eighth Earl of Derby (the son of the James who was beheaded at Bolton), became Lord of Man. The last Lord of Man of the Derby family was James, second son of the above Charles, who succeeded his elder brother William, as Tenth Earl of Derby, in 1702. His nephew William, son of the above William, dying without issue, and before his father, in 1700, and James also dying without issue in 1735, James Murray, Second Duke of Athol, descended from Amelia Sophia, the youngest daughter of James, Seventh Earl of Derby, became Lord of Man in 1736.—(See *Appendix E.*)

Note 64.—"John Christian."

See Note 65, below.

Note 65.—"William Christian, Receiver."

William Christian (or, as the Manx call him "Illiam Dhone," *i.e.*, William the brown haired), was the son of the Deemster, Ewan Christian, of Ronaldsway, near Castletown.

He first appears in history in connection with a petition presented in 1643, to James, Seventh Earl of Derby, who was then in the Island, against Ewan Christian, his father, in behalf of an infant, who was said to have a claim to the estate of Ronaldsway. The prayer of the petition, as stated in the Earl's letter to his son, in Peck's *Desiderata Curiosa* (see vol. iii., *Manx Society*, p. 60), was to the effect "that there might be a fair trial; and when the right was recovered, that I would grant them a lease thereof, &c. This being in 'the tenure of the straw,' and a motion to me which the Deemster may think pleasing, it will doubtless startle him."

It is well known in Manx History that after Goddard Crovan had conquered the Isle of Man, he divided it amongst the natives and those of his followers who chose to remain, on the terms that none should venture to claim their holdings as hereditary property, but simply as tenants at will, to the King. This *stipulation* was known by the name of "the tenure of the straw." Virtually the people had under this tenure held their property, and transmitted it as hereditary; paying to the Lord a small rent, like to a fee-farm in England. The Stanley family claimed by charter all the rights pertaining to any former sovereign, and the Seventh Earl of Derby being dissatisfied with these rents, was anxious to create a tenure more profitable for himself, by substituting leases for three lives. An endeavour was made by the partisans of the Earl to persuade the people that under the "tenure of the straw" having no title deeds, their estates were insecure, but that leases would be equivalent to title deeds, and though nominally for limited periods, made their lands really descendible from father to son. In order to induce them the more readily to surrender their estates, one of the Deemsters made a show of surrendering *his* lands, at the same time entering into a private arrangement with the Earl of Derby, and shortly after obtaining an Act of Tynwald, reinstating him in his possessions.

Ewan Christian, the father of Illiam Dhone, saw very plainly that if the above- mentioned petition were heard, the hearing would probably go against him, since it was promised by the petition that the infant, if successful, would resign his "tenure of the straw," and accept instead a lease of three lives. He therefore decided that it would be best to resign Ronaldsway to his son William, who thereupon accepted the lease, and named his own descendants for the three lives. This proceeding seems to have been so far acceptable to the Earl, on account of the influence of so high an example upon others, that in the year 1648, William Christian was appointed to the post of Receiver-General, and appears to have been taken into the confidence of the Earl and his family. The same year, however, his elder brother John, who had been deputy to his father, the Deemster, was, in consequence of presumed disaffection to the government, confined in Peel Castle, until he "should enter into bonds to be of good behaviour, and not attempt to depart from the Isle without licence." There is no doubt but that the Earl had acted with much severity towards various members of the Christian family, as we have seen in a previous note. He regarded them as treacherous and disloyal, and formenters of sedition, but more particularly as too powerful in the Island, and the greatest obstacles to the carrying out his views respecting the "tenure of the straw." Yet as far as Illiam Dhone himself was concerned, there is no evidence to shew that he was ever treated but with the greatest consideration by the Earl of Derby; and it is plain that he was trusted with the utmost confidence, in all his family matters. On the Earl's leaving the Island, for the last time, to join the standard of Charles the Second, he left Illiam Dhone with the command of the Insular troops, and the care of his Countess and children. He was therefore bound to their defence to the utmost of his ability, by every principle of honor, if not of gratitude.

There is much obscurity still hanging over the acts by which he not only forfeited the confidence reposed in him, but, according to the charge made against him at a later period, on his trial, shewed himself in the eyes of the Derby family a *traitor*.

The general story is, that on the appearance of the Parliamentary troops, under Colonel Duckenfield, at Ramsey, shortly after the execution of the Earl of Derby, at Bolton, he not only prevented the escape of the Countess and her family from the Island, but carried them prisoners to the invading army. Yet it must be said on the other hand, that neither does his name appear amongst those who treated with Colonel Duckenfield, on that occasion, concerning the terms for the surrender of the Island; nor in the accusation upon his trial is any mention made of any such, delivery of the Countess and family, into the enemy's hands.

As far as we can judge by his dying speech, and the counts upon which he was tried and condemned to death, his offence was this: as soon as the execution of the Earl was made known in the Island, a number of the inhabitants banded themselves together to obtain from the Countess a redress of grievances, and more especially of that old one respecting the "tenure of the straw;" and within eight days of the Earl's death, they drew up a petition to the Countess, in which these were embodied. There can be little doubt but that William Christian threw himself at once into their cause, placed himself at their head, and carried the petition to the Countess. This is what was intended in the count that "he was at the head of an insurrection against the Countess of Derby, in 1651, assuming the power unto himself, and depriving her Ladyship, his Lordship, and heirs thereof." According to Illiam Dhone's dying speech, her Ladyship accepted the petition, and entered into terms with the petitioners. Shortly after, on the arrival of the army under Colonel Duckenfield, off Ramsey, Sir Philip

Musgrave, the Governor of the Island, at the head of the Manx troops, marched against him. Negotiations however ensued; a deputation (John Christian, Ewan Curphey, and William Standish) from the Manx to the Parliamentary forces, proceeded on board the fleet to confer upon terms for the surrender of the Island. The only stipulation on the part of the natives was "that they might enjoy their lands and liberties" as formerly they had. Of the subsequent capture of the Countess of Derby, we have no record.

William Christian, as has been before said, was appointed Receiver in 1648. He continued to hold that office under Fairfax, and in addition was appointed in 1656, to succeed Matthew Cadwell, as Governor. Unfortunately the charge of covetousness which was made by the Earl of Derby against his family, appears strongly to attach to him. The receipt of the sequestrated Bishopric, which Fairfax designed for the maintenance of Grammar Schools and increase of stipends of the Clergy, came into his hands; and when Chaloner came into office as Governor, in 1658, it was found that he had embezzled the money. William Christian fled from the Island; and Chaloner not only sequestrated his estates, but imprisoned his elder brother John, for aiding his escape. He was an exile from his native land three years, but his son George was permitted to return to the Island to settle his father's affairs. On the Restoration, Christian went to London, as he says "to get a sight of the King;" but being discovered, he "was arrested for a debt of £20,000, and cast into the Fleet prison, where he continued a year. On gaining at length his liberty, he determined to return to the Isle of Man, under the imagined security of the act of amnesty and indemnity, of King Charles the Second.—(See *Petition of William Christian to Charles the Second*, A.D. 1660, vol. ix., *Manx Society*, p. 151.) By a mandate, however, of Charles, the Eighth Earl of Derby, dated at Lathom, September, 1662, Illiam Dhone was proceeded against for "all his illegal acts at, before, or after 1661;" and the majority of the court, whom we can hardly regard in any other light than as a packed jury, overruling the plea of general amnesty as not availing in the Isle of Man, in case of treason against a member of the reigning family, he was hastily sentenced to be "shot to death, that thereupon his life may depart from his body." The sentence was carried out upon Hango Hill, at the head of Castletown Bay, on the 2nd of January, 1662-3. In answer to his petition to King Charles the Second, an order was issued on Jan. 16th, to the Earl of Derby, for sending up William Christian to be heard before His Majesty and Council, touching the matters wherewith he was charged, but his execution had already taken place.—(See vol. ix., *Manx Society*, p. 152.) His sequestrated estates were however subsequently restored to the family, in which they have continued to the present time: William Watson Christian, Esq., Coroner-General for the Isle of Man, is his lineal representative.

The following entry occurs in the Parish Register of Malew:—"Mr. William Christian of Ronaldsway, late Receiver, was shot to death at Hango Hill, 2nd January, 1602. He died most penitently and most courageously, made a good end, prayed earnestly; and next day was buried in the chancel of Kirk Malew."

By Manxmen his memory is held sacred, as that of one who died in the cause of popular liberty. The documents pertaining to his history, will be given amongst the publications of the *Manx Society*; edited by James Burman, Esq., F.R.A.S., Secretary to H. E. the Lieutenant-Governor of the Isle of Man.

Note 66.—"Robert Tynsley, Atturney-General."

The Tynsleys or Tyldesleys of the Friary, in Kirk Arbory, were long settled in the Isle of Man, and have only, so to speak, recently become extinct. The first of that name to be met with in the Insular Records, is Thurston Tyldesley, Receiver- General of the Isle of Man, in 1532; most probably a scion of the Lancashire family of Tyldesley of Tyldesley, in that county, from whom was sprung Sir T. S. Tyldesley, a Major-General in the Royal Army, who was slain in Wigan-lane, Aug. 25th, 1651, when fighting under James, Seventh Earl of Derby, and who had been with his Lordship a short time before, in the Isle of Man. Another Thomas was Water-Bailiff, in 1632; and Deputy-Governor, in 1640. Richard Tyldesley was one of the Council and Clerk of the Rolls, from 1647 to 1668; and in this latter year is one of the attesting witnesses to the grant of Bishop Barrow, of the estates of Ballagilley and Hango Hill, in Malew Parish, to certain trustees for the founding of an Academic-Students' Fund, which has since grown into King William's College, at Castletown. The other attesting witnesses to the grant, are Henry Nowell, Governor; Richard Stephenson and Thomas Norris, Deemsters. Richard Tyldesley married Isabel, daughter of the above Thomas Norris.

The last of the name was Margaret, daughter of Thomas Tyldesley, of the Friary, and who married at Kirk Arbory, in November, 1795, Benjamin Greetham, Esq., of Liverpool. (P.B.)

Note 67.—"Bangor, Sabal, and St. Trinions."

These Abbey Courts are still held in the Queen's name, and under her proper officers. Anciently the following persons were Barons of the Isle: *viz.*, the Bishop; the Abbot of Rushen; the Prioress of Douglas; the Abbot of Fumess; the Prior of Whithern or St. Trinians, in Galloway; the Abbot of Bangor, in Ireland; the Abbot of Sabal; and the Prior of St. Bede or St. Bees, in Cumberland. In 1422, these Barons were summoned by Sir John Stanley, Lord of the Isle, to come in and do fealty to him. After some demur, the three first submitted, and did their faith and fealty to the Lord; the five latter not being on the Isle, "were called in, but came not."— (See Sacheyerell's *Survey*, p. 67, *Manx Society's* edition.) They were therefore "deemed by the Deemsters" to come in their proper persons within forty days, and if they came not, then all their temporalities were to be seized into the Lord's hands. It appears tolerably certain that the Barons of Bangor, Sabal, and St. Trinians, made no appearance. They were either too far off or too independent. Though we have no record that the Abbot of Furness or the Prior of St. Bees, came in and did fealty, it is not improbable that the latter did so, as we find that in later times the Barony in the Isle of Man attached to that Priory, and which lies in the Parish of St. Maughold, a little to the north of the Dhoon River, on the sea coast, still continued in possession of the fraternity, and it was exchanged with the Christian family in Cumberland, for lands in that county, lying more convenient to St. Bees; the Christian family being possessed of lands both in the Isle of Man and Cumberland. The Barony in the Isle of Man, anciently belonging to St. Bees, thus came into private hands, and appears to be independent of the Insular Courts of Baron, belonging to the Queen. The subscription of the Abbot of Rushen may haye been accepted on behalf of Furness, which was the mother of the Abbey of Rushen.

Note 68.—"The Governour, the two Deemsters."

One clause in the oath of admission of the Governor or Lieutenant-Governor of the Isle of Man, to office, is somewhat remarkable: "You shall truly and uprightly deal between our Sovereign Lady the Queen and her people, and as indifferently betwixt party and party, *as this staff now standeth*, as far as in you lyeth."

In the Lex Scripta of the Isle of Man, we find that very stringent laws were enacted in support of his authority.

"Whoever shall speak any scandalous speech against the Governour, touching either his oath, state of government of the Isle, or what might tend to his defamation, and not be able to prove the same, shall be fined in ten pounds, and have his ears cut off." "If any person rise up against the Governour sitting in any Tynwald Court, wherein he representeth the Lord's person, they are to be deemed traitors, and to be sentenced to death without any inquest passing on them by the Deemster. That they be first drawn after wild horses, then hanged, and afterwards quartered, and their heads struck off and set upon the castle tower, over the town, with one quarter there, the second quarter to be set up in Holland Town (*i.e.*, Holme Town or Peel), the third at Ramsey, and the fourth at Douglas."

The oath administered to the Deemsters on their admission to office, is still more singular: "By this book, and by the holy contents thereof, and by the wonderful works that God hath miraculously wrought in heaven above, and in the earth beneath, in six days and seven nights; I (A.B.), do swear that I will, without respect of favour or friendship, love or gain, consanguinity or affinity, envy or malice, execute the laws of this Isle justly betwixt our Sovereign Lady the Queen and her subjects, within this Isle, and betwixt party and party, as indifferently *as the herring back-bone doth lie in the midst of the fish*. So help me God and by the contents of this book."

Note 69.—"Castle Peel."

Some persons may feel interested in learning how this Castle and Rushen Castle were defended in the olden time. The following are the regulations ordained by an Act of Tynwald, at a Court holden 24th June, 1610:—

"Whereas we are enjoined by the right worshipful John Ireland Esq Lieut & Captn of this Isle by Vertue of our oaths to give notice of our knowledge of the ancient order and

duties observed by the souldiers of the castles of Eushen and
Peele, in our times and memories, and for that purposs wee
twelve, whose names are subscribed, were chosen, whereof
six be sworne souldiers at the castle Rushen, and six at the
castle Peele, upon advised consideration had, wee find and
knowe, That all the ancient orders, customes, and duties to
be performed in the said castles, are extant in the rowles, and
enrolled in the bookes of the statutes of this Isle, and these
which we do add hereafter are, and have beene, customarie
and usual.

"*First*, At the entrance and admittance of any souldier to
either of either of the said castles, the ordinarie oath was to
this purpose:

The oath of a souldier.
"*First*, Our allegiance to our soveraigne, next our faith, fedilitie, and service to the right honoble earls of Derbie and their heires, our duties and our obedience to our lieutenant or cheefe governour and our constable in lawful causes, and noe further.

Souldiers to appear at the castle gates at the sound of the drume.
"*Item*. It hath been accustomed and still continued, that every souldier at the sound of the drume, or ringinge of the alarums bell (the heareing or knowinge of the same) shall forthwith make his present appearance in the gate of either castle, then and there to pforme what shall be enjoyned one them by the lieutnnt, or the constable in his absence.

Night bell to be runge and the guarde set.
"*Item*. It hath been accustomed that night bell should be runge a little after the sun setting, and that by the porter, and constable and his deputie with a sufficient guard to be in the castle, for the saufe keepinge and defence of the same.

Porter to locke the gates.
"*Item*. It hath been accustomed and continued, that the constable or his deputie

should goe with the wardens to the castle gates, and there cause the porter to locke the castle gates, and then the watch to be fourthwith set.

Concerning the porter and watch men. "*Item*. It hath been accustomed, that at either castle there hath beene two standinge porters, who have by course every other weeke held the staff, and given attendance at the gate during one whole yeare, begininge at Michallmas; the said porters to be nominated by the constable, and then allowed by the lieutnnt and governour, and two standinge watchmen in like manner for the nightlie watchinge upon the walls; and every officer, souldier, and servant, is to doe his pettie watch from May till Michallmas.

Pettie watch.

Time of opening gates. "*Item*. It hath been accustomed, that the castle gates should not be opened by any man after lockeinge at night (the governor onelie excepted) until the watchman ringe the day bell, which was to be done so soone as the watchman could pfectli discover the land markes bounded within a mile and a halfe of either castle; which beinge done, the porter was accustomed to goe about the walles, and looke that all things be cleere, and forthwith to returne to the constable or his deputie, and affirme all things to be as the watchman had formerlie spoken to the constable or his deputie.

Souldiers lyingein at both houses. "It hath been accustomed, that the souldiers should ward in the castle gates one day in the weeke, and they of the castle Rushen to lye within the house the night before their warding- day, and the souldiers of the castle Peele to lie in the night before, and the night after, in respect the tyd fallinge out uncertainlie, and for more saufe guard of that castle, beinge nearer to our enemies the Redshankes.

Inner gate locked by one of the wardens.

"It hath been accustomed and still continued, that one of the wardens of the inward ward at castle Rushen shall at night locke inner gate, and keepe the keys thereof to himselfe till morninge, and hath pformed all things therein as constable that night in that ward.

The receiver at Michellmas chuseth a steward.

"It hath been accustomed, that the receiuer of either castle hath at Michellmas made yearly choise of a steward, who hath beene allowed by the lieutnnt or captain for the time beinge.

The souldiers to work the Lord's hay.

"It hath been accustomed and still continued, that the souldiers of either castle have wrought the Lord's hay, whensoever they have been thereunto called.

Two gunners to have either of them apprenticed, and one of them to lie in every night.

"It hath been accustomed, that Mr. Gunner of either castle hath had allowance of an apprentice, and that either himselfe or his apprentice hath every night linen in the said castle.

"Notwithstanding all theise orders, usues, and customes, here set downe, the lieutnnt, captain, or chiefe governor for the time beinge, in his wisdome and accordinge to the necessitie of time set downe orders and decrees for hoth castles in all lawfull causes, and repeal the same againe, which every inferiour officer and soldier is to obey by reason of his oath.

Lieut. to repeal as need re - quireth these or any of the orders

"Thomas Moore, Henerey Garrett, Tho. Whetstone, Tho. Lea, Wm. Lassell, Edward Lucas, Will. Bridgen, John Crellin, Jo. Gauen, Hugh Lambe, Rich. Fisher, John. Colbin.

"John Ire Land, Lieutnnt.

"William Lucas, Wm. Ratcliffe, Tho. Sainsbury, Da. Ewan Xian."

The Crypt, under the choir of Peel Cathedral, was generally used as an Ecclesiastical prison in later times, though the Civil Government had confined prisoners there in earlier periods of Manx history: *viz.*, Thomas, Earl of Warwick, in 1397; and Eleanor Cobham, Duchess of Gloucester, in the 15th century. A view of this Crypt is given in a highly valuable paper, by the Rev. J. L. Petit, M.A., in the *Archaeological Journal*, No. 9, p. 49. This prison-house is referred to, though erroneously stated to be under the burying ground, in the following statement of Manx sufferers, made in the *Abstract of the Sufferings of the People called Quakers*, above referred to in the note upon James Chaloner (No. 2). The Quakers appear to have been equally obnoxious to the Puritans and Episcopalians; but the persecutions which they endured, did not remove them from the Island, as it is recorded that in the days of Bishop Wilson, they were the only dissenters on the Isle of Man, and that he lived on friendly terms with them.

"In 1663, William Callow and Evan Christian, with the said Evan's father, 80 years of age, were committed to Peel Castle, under pretence of absence from Church; but after sixteen days were set at liberty, by order of the Bishop (Isaac Barrow), who came to tho Island to be sworn.

"In 1664, they, with some others, were again imprisoned, by means of an order from two Priests, Judges of the Bishop's Court, in Peel Castle, and kept there from 22nd of March, 1664, till the 7th July, 1667."

The order referred to, was in the following terms:—"We have received orders from our Revd Ordinary, to admonish the Quakers to conform and come to Church, or be committed until they submit to law; and forasmuch as they refuse after several charges and publications in the Parish Church, but continue their meetings and refractoriness to all Government of the Church, and are therefore censured to be committed to St. German's Prison, and there let them remain until orders be given to the contrary, and for so doing, this shall be your discharge.

ROBERT PARR,
JOHN HARRISON.

"P.S. If they refuse to be committed by you, call for the assistance of a Soldier from Capt. Ascoe. Let the Sumner put this in execution immediately."

"Five women were committed: *viz.*, Jane Christian, Jane Kennell (Cannell?), Ann Christian, Mary Callow, and Mary Christian. Of these five women, one was 74 years of age, and her son then in prison. Another, 62 years of age. A third poor woman, with three children; one of them sucking at the breast, she took with her. The fourth, the wife of one not called a Quaker, but having a large family and many children. The fifth, a servant of William Callow, whom they brought away from her sick mistress. These were put in the dungeon under the burying-ground, where the men also were. When the Sumner brought them to the lowest and deepest part of that dismal dungeon, he took off his hat, and very formally pronounced what he called the Bishop's curse; *viz.*, 'I do now before the standers by deliver you up unto St. German's prison, by the law of my Lord Bishop and his Clergy, you being persons cast out of the Church by excommunication; and I do take witness that I do deliver you over from the power of the Bishop and his law, to be and continue the Earl of Derby's prisoners.'

"On the 15th of April 1665, Govr Henry Nowell came to the Castle, and read to the prisoners an order from the Earl of Derby, that they must forthwith he transported into some other land.

"On the 29th of April, Thos. Harrison and John Woods told them they were come by the Deputy-Governor's order, to admonish them to conform to the Church, or else they must be banished forthwith."

It would appear that they were sent to Dublin, and thence sent back to the Isle of Man, as there is extant an order from the Mayor of Dublin, for carrying the prisoners back to the Isle of Man; also, the certificate of the Captain of the vessel, dated 7th October, 1665, that they had been landed at Whitehaven; and a Magistrate's order for carrying them from Whitehaven to the Isle of Man, 4th Nov., 1665, and signed Jas. Lamplugh. It is presumed that they were again committed to Peel Castle, and continued there till 1667. An account of repsurs to Peel Cathedral and Bishop's Court, are given in *Appendix H.*

Note 70.—"Most suitable to its poverty and distance from England."

High testimony has been borne by eminent lawyers and writers, to the excellency of the Manx Legislative Code. "There is one little barren spot," says Sacheverell, "where law and justice, true religion, and primitive integrity, flourished in contempt of poverty, and all things the world calls misfortune." In Ward's *Ancient Records of the Isle of Man*, we read "As no people are more blessed, so none are more happy and content than the Manx, under their venerable laws, and simple, primitive, I had almost said patriarchal constitution. Our orderly state was well described to me by a traveller, I accidentally met, two years since, on the Continent. 'I have lately been visiting,' he said, 'the Isle of Man; and I found there what I did not believe existed, a legislature governing wholly and solely for the public good; a people desiring nothing less than to send Members to Parliament; and a Bishop, happy in his freedom from the House of Lords.'"

Coke, in his *Fourth Institute*, chap. 69, says "The laws are more strictly carried into execution, and with less trouble, than in any other place in the world."

Crutwell, in his preface to *Bishop Wilson's Works*, states in reference to the Manx Ecclesiastical Code (the Canons of the Manx Church, which are also Statute law), that Lord Chancellor King was so much pleased with these Constitutions, that he said "If the ancient discipline of the Church were lost, it might be found in all its purity in the Isle of Man."

Note 71.—"Hardly deserveth a chapter by itself."

The Act of Revestment, 1765, and its completion by the entire transfer of all the rights and privileges of the Duke of Athol, to the British Crown, in 1825, leading to the suppression of smuggling, a great impetus was thus given to legitimate trade, and the development of the great natural resources of the Isle of Man. Its trade now fully deserves a chapter in any history of it which may be written. The present exports of grain, green crop, and cattle, are very extensive, reaching from 12,000 to 15,000 tons of potatoes per annum, more than 20,000 quarters of wheat, besides a proportionate amount of barley and oats, chiefly grown in the upland districts. The cattle, horses, pigs, poultry, butter, and eggs, find a ready market in Liverpool and Whitehaven. The Manx, however, continue to look to their fisheries for some of the largest returns. The average annual produce of the fisheries, is upwards of £60,000. In herrings alone, besides those consumed fresh, both on the Island and the surrounding countries, there are about 40,000 barrels annually cured, the price of which paid to the fishermen, is on an average £1.10s.0d. per barrel. To this must be added the cod, ling, salmon, and lobster fisheries. The export of minerals—copper, lead, zinc, silver, and iron—reaches a large amount; the Island itself being one of the richest mining districts in the United Kingdom. The produce of the mines (as was stated in *Note* 17) has of late years reached the total of 2,600 tons of lead; copper 350 tons; zinc 3,181 tons; iron 1,650 tons; silver 57,000 ounces. The stone quarries of Poolvash, Scarlet, Spanish Head, and Mica Mount near Foxdale, have afforded many hundred of tons of marble, limestone, flagstone, and granite. There is also a very considerable quantity of limestone burnt into lime, at Ballahott and Port St. Mary. The Manx have in addition manufactures of sail cloth, ropes and nets, woollen goods, paper, soap, and farina. The amount of trade carried on now by the Isle of Man, may be judged of by the fact that the import duties (which are by no means heavy) reach the figure of upwards of £32,000 per annum.

Note 72.—"At Lanquet Point."

This Fort was erected by James, the Seventh Earl of Derby, on St. Michael's Isle, at the western extremity of Langness, in 1645, as appears by a record under that date, in the *Liber Scaccar*, preserved in Rushen Castle, which states that on the 26th of April, of that year, it was named Derby Fort, in honour of Charlotte, Countess of Derby, daughter of Claude de Tremouille, Duke of Touars; who, on the corresponding day of the previous year, had beat off the enemy from their attack on Lathom House. Over the doorway may still be seen an Earl's coronet, with the half obliterated date 1645. For an account of the miraculous escape of James, Seventh Earl of Derby, when leaving this Fort in 1650, see *Note* 5 supra; and my *Story of Rushen-Castle and Rushen Abbey*, p. 35.

Note 73.—"The Castle of Rushen."

The Castle of Rushen was according to Manx tradition, founded by the Danish Guthred or Godred, the son of Orry, in 960. A portion of an oak beam, which was taken down in repairing the Castle, some years ago, and is still preserved, bears the date 947 (which was the year of Guthred's accession), and some seemingly maesogothic characters.

Considerable doubt is thrown upon the assertion that this inscription was contemporaneous with the building, from the circumstance that Arabic numerals were hardly introduced into Europe, so early as the 10th century. The Keep, as far as we can judge by the architecture, is of the 12th century. The Castle is in an admirable state of preservation. Subterranean chambers were discovered very recently, during certain alterations which were made last year.

Note 74.—"There is a Block House at Duglas."

The Block House at Douglas stood at the extremity of the Pollock rock, near the entrance of the harbour of Douglas. A view of it is given in *Feltham's Tour*, vol. vi., *Manx Society*, It was a Lock-up at the beginning of the present century, but was taken down in harbour improvements, by an order of the Insular Legislature, in 1818. Formerly watch and ward used to be kept in this building, for the security of the Port of Douglas.

Note 75.—"A Fort in the middest of the Island."

Probably this was an earthwork, of which remains exist at Ballachurry, in Andreas parish, not far from St. Jude's Church. It consists of an internal rectangular area, 144 feet long, by 120 wide, at the corners of which are four bastions, the tops of which are about 48 feet square, all constructed of the earth which has been thrown up out of the ditch surrounding the encampment.

APPENDICES

APPENDIX A.
GENEALOGICAL TABLE OF THE FAMILY OF ALAN, LORD OF GALLOWAY.

ALAN,* Lord of Galloway, died in 1233: he married thrice, and in addition to his legitimate family, he had an illegitimate only son, called Thomas Mac Dhu Alan.

By his first wife, (name unknown).

Thomas Mac Dhu Alan, married the daughter of Reginald, (bastard son of Godred the Black) who usurped the Kingdom of Man, in 1187.§ Fordun states that the people of Galloway were indignant because they could not obtain that "Thomas filius naturalis Alani, exhereditatis tribus filiabus suis heredibus legitimis, fieret herest eorum Bominus."

Helena, married to Roger de Quincy, Earl of Winchester, and High Constable of Scotland, in right of his wife.

Thomas died without issue.

William Comyn, Earl of Menteith.

By his second wife, Margaret, dau. of David, Earl of Huntingdon.

Christian married in 1236, to William de Fortibus, Earl of Albemarle. No issue.

Devorgille married in 1233, to John de Baliol, of Barnard Castle.

Marian (or Mary)† married to John Comyn (the first Red Comyn).

John Comyn, Lord of Badenoch (the Black Comyn).§

Alexander Comyn.

Robert Comyn.

John Comyn (the Second Red Comyn) slain by Robert Bruce, 1306-7.

Helen, I or Ela, married to Alan de Zouche, of Ashby.

By his third wife, dau. of Henry de Lacy.

No issue.

Four daughters, the third of whom was married to‡ Alaster de Ergadia, lord of Lorn

John de Ergadia.

Margaret, married to William de Ferrers, Vith Earl of Derby. For a short time till his death High Constable of Scotland, in right of his wife.

Elizabeth, married to Alexander Comyn, Earl of Buchan # and High Constable of Scotland, in right of his wife.

William Comyn,# Provost of the Canonry of St. Andrew's.

Five daughters. (See Appendix D.)

John Comyn, Earl of Buchan.

Alexander Comyn. Earl of Buchan.

William Comyn.#

Margaret Comyn married to John de Ross, son of the Earl of Ross.

Alice Comyn, married to Henry de Beaumont, Lord of Man.¶

* Son of Roland, Lord of Galloway. Roland, Lord of Galloway, married Ela or Helen de Moreville, sister of William de Moreville,High Constable of Scotland. The office of High Constable was hereditary in the family of the De Morevilles, and on the death of William, in 1196, went to Roland, in right of his wife; and then upon Alan's death, to her eldest grand-daughter Helena, and from her to the husbands of her daughters Margaret ard Elizabeth. Helena de Quincy's portion seems to have consisted of the estates and honors of the de Morevilles, whilst Galloway was reserved for the family of Margaret, of Scotland, the second wife of Alan.

† Shaw's History of Province of Moray. See Note 66 supra. The Galloway estates which were large, possessed by the Red Comyn, seem to have come to the family through this lady.

‡ See Appendix C.

§ William Comyn, Earl of Buchan, put down the rebellion of Gillespoc, Earl of Moray, about 1229; and Alexander the Second gave him as a reward, the territory of Badenoch, for his second son Walter: who, on his death, passed it on to the next second son of the family, viz., John, the Black Comyn.-(See *Appendix D.*)

See Appendix D.

¶ See Appendix B and D.

APPENDIX B.
GENEALOGICAL TABLE OF THE ERGADIA FAMILY.

SHOMHAIRLE (or SOMERLED) MACGILBERT, Thane of Argyle;
married for his second wife Affreca, illegitimate daughter
of Olave Kleining, King of Man, the father of Godred.-
(See Appendix C)

Dugall, Lord of Lorn, made
king of the Isles in 1155.

Reginald, inherited Lorn on the
death of his brother Dugall,
but at his demise, it reverted
to Dugall's sons.

Aongus, slain in 1210 with
his three sons. (See
Chronicon Manniae).

Olave.

Dugall Scrag. Duncan. Haco Uspac, killed
founder of the priory in Bute, 1230.
of Ardchattan in Lorn.

Roderic
(chief of Clan Rory),
called Dominus de
Kyntire.

Donald
(chief of Clan Donald)

Dugall
(chief of Clan Dugall)

Angus Moir,
a member of the
convention at Scone

Duncan.

Eugene or Ewen de Ergadia, Lord of Lorn.
On account of his adherence to Norway,
Alexander II. of Scotland made an ex
expedition against him in 1249, but died
at Kerreray

Dugall.   Alan.
King of the Isles. Bound himself
No male issue. at Scone, 1284.
                 to recognise
                 the Maid of Norway

Alexander (or Alaster) de Ergadia, Mal-
colm

Mary, married to Reginald (Olavesen)
king of Man, who was slain by Ivar
in 1249. After Reginald's death she
married Maltise. Earl of Strathern.
by whom she had a son Maltise. She
was styled Countess of Strathern.
and Queen of Man.

Mary, wife of John de Waldeboef, was
daughter of this Mary by Reginald.
King of Man.

A daughter,
married to Alexander
of the Isles

John de Ergadia espoused the cause of
his cousin John (the second Red
Comyn, who was murdered by Bruce
in 1306.)-(See Appendix D.) He
had great possessions in the Isle of
Man, from which he was driven out
by Bruce in 1313, and which he did
not recover till 1340. He is the
ancestor of the Macdougalls of Lorn.

Thane of Glasserie and Knapdale.
Lord of Lorn; married the third
daughter of John Comyn (the first Red Comyn)+

Duncan de Ergadia, the lord Dingawi
Macdoual of the Chronicon Mannia.
who defended Rushen castle against
king Robert Bruce. in 1313.

The Appendix B table is taken chiefly from Skene's *Highlanders of Scotland.*

On the death of Ewen de Ergadia, [the father of Mary the wife of Reginald (Olavesen), see Appendix C,] the clan Siol Cuinn, of which he had been the head, was divided into three clans, the chiefs of which were the three sons of Reginald Macgilbert, younger brother of Dugall, the son of Somerled. It will be seen by the above table that Ewen de Ergadia, the father of Mary the wife of Reginald King of Man, was second cousin, once removed, to Alaster de Ergadia, who married a daughter of the first Red Comyn.

In the Chartulary of Cupar, 1253-70, appears the name of Alexander de Ergadia, son of Duncan, son of Dugall, son of Reginald, as a witness.—(See also *Appendix D.*)

APPENDIX C.

GENEALOGICAL TABLE OF GODRED THE BLACK (OLAVESON) KING OF MAN AND THE ISLES.

GODRED came to the throne of Man and the Isles in 1154; married Fingala, daughter of Mc Lotlen King of Ireland, died in 1187; and left the throne to his younger son Olave, who, of all his children, was alone considered legitimate. (See Chronicon Manniæ, Anno MCLXXXVII.)

Reginald. usurped the Kingdom of Man and the Isles in 1187, which he kept from his brother Olave till 1226 Made surrender of his kingdom to the Pope, 1219. Was slain in the battle of Tynwald Hill.

Feb. 14, 1229. He married the daughter of a nobleman of Kintyre.

Guin. Leandres.

- Godred I Don. assassinated in the Lewis in 1236.
- Daughter married to Thomas Mac Dhu Alan. son of Alan Lord of Galloway.

Ivar

Affreca. married to John de Conroy, Earl of Ulster, on May 21st, 1237.

Olave (the Black) was kept out of his kingdom by Reginald. till 1226. Died 1237. Married twice. Ist wife Joan, the daughter of a nobleman of Kintyre. IInd. Christina, dau. of Ferquhard, Earl of Ross.

Leod.

- **Harold**, born 1223. Came to the throne of Man 1237. Married Cecilia. dau. of Haco. king of Norway. Drowned in the Somburg Rost in 1248. See Chronicon Manniae

- **Reginald.** Came to the throne in 1249. Was slain on the 6th of May, of the same year, near Trinity Church, Rushen, by the knight Ivar, the grandson of the usurper Reginald. He married Mary, dau. of Eugene de Ergadia, who afterwards became countess of Strathern by marriage with Malise, Earl of Strathern. See Appendix B.

- **Affreca.** Claimed the Isle of Man on the death of Magnus and made petition for it to Baliol, who refusing her, was cited to appear before Edward I, at the King's Bench, in 1293. She married Sir Simon de Montacute, and made over to him her rights by a charter which is dated 1305.

- **Magnus.** Came to the throne of Man in 1252; did homage for it to Alexander III of Scotland, in 1263, and died, without issue, in Rushen Castle, Nov. 24th, 1265. See Chronicon Mananiae. He was the last of the kings of Man, of the male race of Godard Crovan.

Harold, seized the Isle of Man in 1250.

Ivar, the knight who murdered Reginald (Olaveson) in 1249. He opposed the landing of the Scots under John Comyn + Alexander Stewart, and was slain in the battle of Ronaldsway, in 1270. See Chronicon Manniae, and Appendix D.

Mary, married to John de Waldeboef.

William de Waldeboef.
|
John de Waldeboef, petitioned Edward Ist in 1345, for the land of Man, and was suffered to be heard in the King's Bench. See Rot. Parl. 33 Ed. Ist.

Mary de Waldeboef, said to have been married to Sir William de Montacute. See Sacheverell's Short Survey of the Isle of Man, p. 60. = Sir William de Montacute, obtained the Isle of Man from the Scots, in 1305, and mortgaged it to Anthony Bee, Bishop of Durham, and Patriarch of Jerusalem.
|
Sir William de Montacute, Ist earl of Salisbury, re-conquered the Isle of Man from the Scots, in 1343, and was crowned king of Man in 1344, and died the same year.
|
Sir William de Montacute, IInd earl of Salisbury, succeeded his father as King of the Isle of Man in 1344, and sold his rights in 1393, to Scrope, Earl of Wiltshire.*

* "Wilhelmus le Scropp emit de Domino Wilhelmo Montacuto Insulam Eubouiae id est Manniae. Est nempe jus ipsius Insulae ut quisquis illius sit Dominus Rex vocetur, cui etiam fas est corona aurea coronari." See Sacheverell's Short Survey of the Isle of Man, p. 61. The Earl of Wiltshire having been defeated by Henry Duke of Lancaster (Henry IV), at Raglan Castle, in 1399, was beheaded without attainder. On this ground Mr. Simon Thomas Scrope, of Danby, in Yorkshire, is now (1864) claiming the Earldom. Henry IV professed to make grants of the Isle of Man, first to Henry Percy, Earl of Northumberland, and then in 1406 to Sir John Stanley.

APPENDIX D.

GENEALOGICAL TABLE SHEWING THE INTEREST OF THE COMYNS AND BEAUMONTS IN THE ISLE OF MAN.

ROBERT DE COMINES,* CUMIN ox COMYN:
Came into England with William the Conqueror, and was created Earl and Governor of Northumberland, 1068.-(See Hume's History of England.) He was slain in battle, near Durham. Jan. 28. in 1069.1 when endeavouring to subjugate the North of England. His name is on the Roll of Battle Abbey.

John de Comyn.

William de Comyn, Chancellor to King David I., in 1133.

William de Comyn, married A.D. 1141, Maud. dau. of Thurstan Banaster, subsequently married to William de Hastings. A.D. 1158.

Richard de Comyn (called the Chancellor's nephew), married Hexilda, the grand-daughter of Donald Bane, king of Scotland, and younger brother of Malcom Cean Mohr. He succeeded to the family estates in Northumberland, and was Lord of the Castle of Northallerton, Yorkshire, in 1144; and died circa 1189.-(See Sir H. Nicholas's Historical Peerage.)

John Coryyn, who died circa 1159. vit. pat.-(See Kelso Chartulary.)

William de Comyn (Earl of Buchan il 1189), was a noted diplomatist, and went to England on an embassy from William the Lion, in 1200. to congratulate king John, of England, on his accession. In the year 1212 he was appointed Guardian of Moray, and towards the close of the reign of king William (1209), and during the greater part of that of Alexander the IInd. he held the office of Great Justiciar of the kingdom of Scotland. He maintained the peace of the Kingdom during the rebellions which broke out in Moray in 1212 and 1229. He died in 1233, aged 78.+ He married twice, and at the beginning of the 13th century (in 1209), became Earl of Buchan, in right of his second wife Marjorie, only daughter and heiress of Fergus, Earl of Buchan. He founded the Abbey of Deir, 1218, and was buried there.

Odo Clomyn, an Ecclesiastic

Ydonea Comyn, married to Adam Fitz Gilbert, ancestor of the Hamiltons.

By his first wife. Matilda Urquhart (daughter of Frederic Urquhart by his first wife Coetissa, daughter of Bancho, Thane ofIochaber).-(See Tre of the Royal House of Stewart.)

By his second wife Marjorie, countess of Buchan, who died circa 1237-8.

Margaret Comyn, married Bartime Setoun, ancestor of the Earls of

Walter I Comyn. created Lord of Badenoch, in 1229. Married

Alexander Comyn, Earl of Buchan. He was not designated Earl of Buchan till 1243, after the death of his mother. He married

William Comyn.

Fergus Comyn.

Elizabeth, married William. Earl of Marr.

Richard Comyn, died in 1249.

John Comyn (the

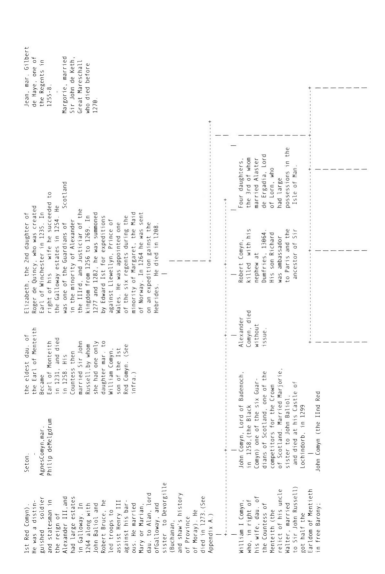

1st Red Comyn). He was a distinguished soldier and statesman in the reign of Alexander III, and had large estates in Galloway. In 1264 along with John Baliol and Robert Bruce, he led troops to assist Henry III against his barous. He married Mary or Marian, dau. to Alan, lord ofGalloway, and sister to Devorgille (Buchanan, and Shaw's history of Province of Moray). He died in 1273. (See Appendix A.)

Seton.

Agnes Comyn, mar. Philip deMelgdrum

the eldest dau. of the Earl of Menteith Became Earl of Monteith in 1231, and died in 1258. His Countess then married Sir John Russell, by whom she had one only daughter mar. to William Comyn, son of the 1st Red Comyn. (See infra.)

Elizabeth, the 2nd daughter of Roger de Quincy, who was created Earl of Winchester in 1235. In right of his wife he succeeded to the Galloway estates in 1254. He was one of the Guardians of Scotland in the minority of Alexander the IIIrd, and Justiciar of the kingdom from 1256 to 1269. In 1277 and 1282, he was summoned by Edward Ist for expeditions against Llewellyn, Prince of Wales. He was appointed one of the six regents during the minority of Margaret, the Maid of Norway. In 1264 he was sent on an expedition against the Hebrides. He died in 1268.

Jean, mar. Gilbert de Haye, one of the Regents in 1255-8.

Margorie, married Sir John de Keth, Great Mareschall who died before 1278

William I Comyn, who, in right of his wife, dau. of the Countess of Menteith (the relict of his uncle Walter, married to Sir John Russell) got half the Earldom of Mentieth in free Barony;

John Comyn, Lord of Badenoch, in 1258, (the Black Comyn) one of the six Guardians of Scotland, one of the competitors for the Crown of Scotland. Married Marjorie, sister to John Baliol, and died at his Castle of Lochindorb, in 1299

Alexander Comyn, died without issue.

Robert Comyn, killed with his nephew at Dumfries, 13064. His son Richard was ambassador to Paris and the ancestor of Sir

Four daughters, the 3rd of whom married Alaster de Ergadia, lord of Lorn, who had large possessions in the Isle of Man.

John Comyn (the IInd Red

APPENDIX D. ((Continued)
GENEALOGICAL TABLE SHEWING THE INTEREST OF THE COMYNS AND BEAUMONTS IN THE ISLE OF MAN.

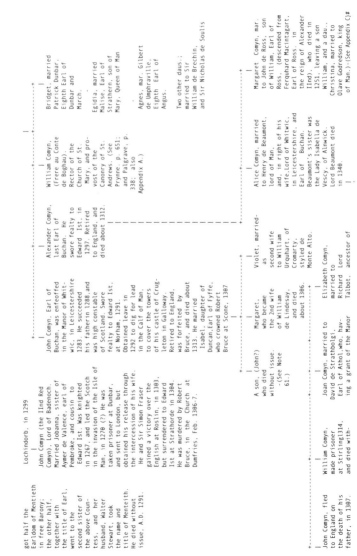

Lochindorb, in 1299

John Comyn (the IInd Red Comyn), Lord of Badenoch. Married Jobanna, sister of Aymer de Valence, earl of Pembroke, and cousin to Edward Ist. Was knighted in 1267. and led the Scotch in the invasion of the Isle of Man, in 1278 (?) He was taken prisoner at Dunbar, and sent to London, but obtained his release through the intercession of his wife. He and Sir Simon Fraser gained a victory over the English at Roslin, in 1383. but surrendered to Edward Ist at Strathorde in 1304. He was murdered by Robert Bruce, in the Church at Dumfries, Feb. 1386-7.

Alexander Comyn, last Earl of Buchan. He swore fealty to Edward Ist. in 1297. Retired to England, and died about 1312.

William Comyn, (Frere au Conte de Boghau). Rector of the Church of St. Mary, and pro-vost of the Canonry of St. Andrews. (See Pryune. p. 651; and Palgrave, p. 338; also Appendix A.)

Bridget, married Patrick Dunbar, Eighth Earl of Dunbar and March.

Egidia, married Malise, Earl of Strathern, son of Mary, Queen of Man

Agnes, mar. Gilbert de Umphraville, Eighth Earl of Angus.

Two other daus.; married to Sir William de Brechin, and Sir Nicholas de Soulis.

John Comyn, Earl of Buchan, was enfeoffed in the Manor of Whit-wic, in Leicestershire 1283. He succeeded his father in 1288, and was high constable of Scotland. Swore fealty to Edward Ist, at Norham, 1291. Obtained leave in 1292 to dig for lead in the Calf of Man. to cover the towers of his castle of Crug-leton in Galloway. Retired to England, was forfeited by Bruce, and died about 1313. He married Isabell. daughter of Duncan.earl of fyffe, who crowned Robert Bruce at Scone, 1387

Alice Comyn, married to Henry de Beaumont, lord of Man, and, in right of his wife, Earl of Whitwic, in leicestershire. and Earl of Buchan. Beaumont's sister was the Lady Isabella de Vescy, of Alnwick. Lord Beaumont died in 1348

Margaret Comyn, mar. to John de Ross, son of William, Earl of Ross. (descended from Ferquhard Macintagart, Earl of Ross. in the reign of Alexander IInd), who died in 1251, leaving a son William, and a dau. Christina, married to Olave Godredson, king of Man.)-(See Appendix C)#

A son. (John?) who died without issue. (See Note 61.)

Margaret, who became the 2nd wife of Lindsay, and died about 1386.

Violet, married as second wife to William Urquhart, of Cromarty, styled de Monte Alto.

William Comyn, made prisoner at Stirling1314, and died with-

Joan Comyn, married to David de Strathbolgi, Earl of Athol,who, hav-ing a grant of the Manor

Elizabeth Comyn, married to Richard Lord Talbot, ancestor of

got half the Earldom of Mentieth in free Barony; the other half, together with the title of Earl. went to the second sister of the above Coun-tess, and her husband, Walter Stewart, took the name and title of Mentieth. He died without issue, A.D. 1291.

John Comyn, fled to England on the death of his father, in 1387.

He died in 1325. By his wife Margaret, he had one only son.	out issue.-See Burke'sExtinct Peerage.	of Chilham, was summoned to Parliament. as a baron. 1322. and died in 1335.§	the Earls of Shrewsbury. See Jacob's Peerage.
	David de Strathbolgi (Earl of Athol) 2nd baron, being a minor of 3 years of age. on the death of his father was put under the guardianship of Henry de Beaumont. He inherited the lands of his uncle, John Comyn, and also lands as one of the co-heirs of Aymer de Valence, earl of Pembroke.		
Adomar Aymer Comyn, who died in 1316, vit. pat. By an inquest held that same year, his aunts, Joan and Elizabeth, were named his heirs. (See Historic Peerage of England, by Sir H. Nicholas, p. 123; see also Note 61 infra	John de Beaumont (second baron Beaumont, but never entitled Earl of Buchan, or Lord of Man). was summoned to Parliament 25th Feb. 1342. He married Lady Alinore Plantagenet, 5th daughter of Henry, Earl of Lancaster. and great grand-daughter of Henry IIIrd. and died in 1342, leaving only one child, a son Henry, from whom are descended-the Beaumonts of Coleorton, in Leicestershire; the Beaumonts of Stoughton Grange; the Beaumonts of Burton on-Trent; and the Beaumonts of Weduesbury, Staffordshire.	Elizabeth Beaumont. married to Nicholas de Audley, son and heir to James Lord Audley, of Heley. No issue. --(See Burke's Extinct Peerage.)	Isabel Beaumont 5th dau..married to Henry Plantagenet. Duke of Lancaster. | Blanche Plantagenet. mar. John of Gaunt. | KING HENRY IV.
		Three other daughters.	

* According to Sir Bernard Burke, John, Count de Comyn, and Baron of Tonsberg, in Normandy, was the son of Baldwin, a distin- guisbed Soldier of the Cross ; and grandson of Charles, Due d'Ingeheim, fifth son of the Emperor Charlemagne. He was the founder of the noble house of Blois, in France; and progenitor of the noble families of De Burg and Burke, in Ireland. John, Count de ('omyn, and Baron of 'Tonsberg, had two sons: (1.) Harlowen de Burg, who married Arlotta, mother of William the Conqueror; (2.) Eustace, Baron de Tonsberg. Harlowen (who died before his father), left, by his wife Arlotta, two sons: (1.) Odo, Bishop of Bayeux, created Earl of Kent, in 1068; (2.) Robert, Count de Moreton, created Earl of Cornwall, 1068. Both the sons were with their half-brother, William the Conqueror, at the battle of Hastings.

Chronica de Melros, A.D. MLXIX. " Comes Robertus Cumine cum DCCtis fere viris apud Dunelmum a Norhimbris occiditur." (See also Speed's History of England.) Chronica de Melros, A.D. MCCXXIII. "Obiit Wilhelmus Cumin Comes de Buquhan, Abbatie de Dere Fund ator."

§ David de Strathbolgie was killed in the forest of Kilbaine, with Walter and Thomas Comyn, in 1335. His Countess Katharine and her young son, aged three years, were beseiged in the castle of Lochindorb, from Nov., 1336, to August, 1336, when Edward III. came to her relief in person.

++ The Earl of Dunbar and March, writing to King Henry IV, in 1400, says: Gif Dame Alice the Beaumont, was your Grand Dame [Great Grandmother (?)] Dame Marjorie Cumyn was my Grand Dame on t'other side; so that I am bot of the feirde degree of kyn to you. " (See Pinkerton's History.) Margaret Ross may have married secondly the Earl of Dunbar and March; and her lands being given to, her first husband, may have settled on his heirs. Or, the Earl of Dunbar and March, in 1400, may have made a mistake in a generation, as he was descended from Bridget, eldest daughter of Alexander Comyn, Earl of Buchan, and aunt to Alice Beaumont and Margaret Ross.

APPENDIX E.
GENEALOGY OF THE DERBY FAMILY AND HOUSE OF ATHOL, SO FAR AS RELATES TO THE SEPARATION OF THE ISLE OF MAN FROM THESE FAMILIES.

```
JAMES, LORD STRANGE, Lord of Man,        =    Charlotte, daughter of Claude de la Tremouille
summoned to Parliament 3 Charles I.,          afterwards (Duke of Thouars), who defended Lathom
Seventh Earl of Derby, and beheaded at        House against the Parliamentarians, in 1644.
Bolton, in Lancashire, for his loyalty,
anno 1651.
   |                                             |                |              |                      |
Charles, who  = Helena Rupa,  Edward, died   William, died  Mary, married to   Katherine, mar.     Amelia = John, Third
succeeded     | a German     without issue.  without issue. the Earl of        to the Marquis      Sophia.| Earl of Athol.
him as Eighth | Lady.                                        Strafford,and left of Dorchester,
Earl of Derby.|                                              no issue.          and left no issue.
   |                                                                                  |
   |          |           |                  |                       |          Charlotte, mar.    And other
William    = Eliz. dau.  Robert,          James, the Tenth Mary, daughter  Charles,  to Thomas,      children,
who        | of         died             Earl of Derby,   and sole heir to died      Lord Colchester, who died
succeeded  | Thomas,    without          succeeded in 1782, Sir William     without   who died         young without
in 1672, as| Earl of    issue.           and gave the Act  Morley, of       issue.    without issue.   issue.
Ninth Earl | Ossory.                     of Settlement in  Halnaccar.
of Derby.  |                             1703, to the Isle of
                                         Man. He was the
                                         last Earl of that
                                         family which had
                                         governed the Isle
                                         for more than 300
                                         years
```

John = Henrietta
Earl of
Anglesea.

John, = Katherine,
first Duke | daughter of
of Athol. | Wm. & Ann.
| Duke and
| Duchess of
| Hamilton.

One son
who died
without
issue.

One son,
who died
without
issue.

Elizabeth
died
without
issue.

John,
Lord
Ashburnham,
her
second husband.

One son,
who died
without
issue.

James,
second
Duke of
Athol,
became Lord
of Man
in 1735.

Charles, Lt.-General of
Prince Charles'
army in 1745.
Attainted, and
died in Holland
11th Oct. 1760.

George, died 1720

Amelia, sole
daughter and
heiress of James
Murray, of
Glencarse and
Strowan.

Basil,
died
young

William,
attainted for
rebellion,
and died in
the Tower,
1747.

John
Marquis
Tullibane,
who fell
in battle at
Malplaquet,
in 1709.

One daughter
only, who
died without
issue.

One daughter
only, who
died without
issue.

Charlotte, Baroness = John, Third Duke of Athol, who
Strange, only child,   succeeded in 1764, and sold his
married to her cousin.   rights in the Isle of Man A.D.
                          1765, to the BRITISH CROWN.

Ten other children.

see Atholl Lords

APPENDIX F.
(See Note 37 supra.)

————

(*From Episcopal Register.*)
Bi'pps Corte, ye 26th Mar., 1660.

It is Refferred unto Parson Robt Parr and Sr Robt Allen, ioynetly to examine, trye, and Inquire into ye abilities iudgemt and conversac'on of Mr. Henry Harrisson whether he is competently quallified to be addmitted unto ye degrees of Deacon and minister, and to certifye me thereof without delay. Dated supra.

JAMES CHALONER.

————

Hoble Govenor all due respect prmised, &c., I have sevrall times since Mr. Henry Harison's return from the Colledge, examined, tried, and enquired into ye Abilities and judgmt of him, and conceive him to be as competently quallified to be admitted unto ye degree of deacon and minister as any of or nation, his coversacon evrsince answerable to ye said Calinge.

Ita testor,
RO. PARRE.

————

Sr

That wch doth most encourage me to comende unto yr Honr Mr. Henry. Harrison afour named, is not his schollershippe: for wch I holde him to be ablre then some that have taken that callinge of the Ministery of ye Gosple, (that

Greate worke spoken of by St. Paul, 2 Cor., ii., 16) alreadie; but that wch doth most enbolden me (I say) is the testimonie of his own mouth, wch he saith hath p'ceeded from a good, & intire conscience: that he holdeth himselfe quallified & called by God, & that he doth intende by the helpe of the Almightie for to discharge the same as that his whole endeavour shall be, as much as in him lieth to advance the Glory of God, and to bringe home many sheepe to his folde, many soules to his Kingdome, wch I praye that he may doe; & if otherwise, I must, & will laye the sin to his owne charge. This Sr wth my Humble & due Respects, I Recomende unto yr Honr acknoweleginge myselfe

Y' Honrs in all Xtian & Ministeriall dutie & service,
March 27th, 1660.   RO. ALLEN.

War.: ye ⎫
27 Mar., ⎬ I am very well satisfied wth ye testimonie herein had, and doe ordr yt ye Regr doe Record these
1660.   ⎭ testimonialls.

JAMES CHALONER.

Hoble Governr

We of the Clergie of this Isle whose names are subscribed, being mett this day at the p'ish Church of K. Marowne, in reall obedience to yor honrs comands to the ordinac'on of Mr. Henry Harrison, Deacon and Preist, in regard yor hors comisaion is directed to all ye Clergie, and none appeared but or selves, under favour of yor hor wee have not attempted to p'ceed in ye Ordinac'on being a worke of soe high a calling untill all or ye major p'te of the Clergie meet upon that service, craveing yor hors pardon herein, we reast

March 4th, 1660.   hoble
                                    yor hors humble servants,
                                              RO. PARRE,

The genrall sumnr hath appeared to sweare that all
the Clergie had notice
and charge to appeare this
day.

    Keepe this upon Record,

        JAMES CHALONER.

WILL. OATS,
THO. HARRISON,
PATRICK THOMPSON,
JOHN CRELLIN,
ED. CROWE,
THO. PARR,
JOHN WOODS.

————

INSULA }
MONAE }

B'ipps Court, May 9th, 1660.

L. S.

Thease are to require and injoyne any three
of the Ministars on the North side of the Isle, to
conveine themselves upon the 15th day of this
instant may by the hour of tenn of the clock at
the furthest, in the aforenoone of the same day,
of which Number, pson Sr Robt Parr is to be
one, for the ordaineing of Mr. Henrey Hairison,
Deacon and Preist, for wch this shall be your
Warrant; given under my hand and Scale of Armes the day
and yeare above written.

        JAMES CHALONER.

————

Wee, whose names are subscribed, a select number of the
Clergie of this Isle required, and injoyned by or hoble
governors comission (bearing date 9th of May), to convenie
or selves upon the 16th day of the sd month, for the ordaining
of Mr. Henry Harison, Deacon and Priest. In obedience unto
his hors comission, and in case of necessitie to suplie the cure
of Kk German of Peele (voyd by the abnegac'on of Mr. George
Harison), Wee have this day prfixed met in the p'ish Church

of Jurby, and in solemlie manner after examinacon of the said Mr. Henry Harisons abilite and sufficientie for Liffe and doctrine, to undertake the cure of souls we have Ordained him deacon and full minister by exhortac'on praying and imposition of hands according to the Apostles rule 1 Tim. iv., 14, desiring that the said comission and or p'ceedings thereupon be recorded for or Discharge. Dat. maij 150° 1660°.

RO. PARRE,

JOHN HARRISONE,

ED. CROWE,

JOH. HUDDLESTONE.

Let ye comission and ye proceedings thereupon bee recorded. 16. May 1660.

JAMES CHALONER.

————

APPENDIX G.

(See Note 38 supra.)

————

Festivities at Rushen Castle in 1643-4.

The right hoble James Earle of Derbie and his right hoble Countesse invited all the Officere' Temparall and Spirituall The Cleargie the 24 Keyes of the Isle the Crowners with all theire wives & likewise the best sort of the rest of the Inhabitance of the Isle to a great maske; where the right hoble Charles lo. Strange wth his traine the right hoble Ladies wth theire attendance were most gloriously decked with silver and gould broidered workes & most Costly ornaments bracelletts on there hands chaines on there neckes Jewels on there foreheads, earrings in there eares & Crownes on there heads

and after the maske to a feast which was most royall &
plentifull wth shuttinge of ornans &c And this was on the
twelfth day (or last day) in Christmas in the yeare 1644. All
the men just wth the earle and the wives with the Countesse
likewise there was such another feast that day was twelve
moneth at night beinge 1643.

pr me
THO PARRE Vicr
of Malew.

————

APPENDIX H
(See Note 69 supra.)

————

(From Episcopal Register.)

Havinge perused and considered the Severall Answers and
Returns made by the respective Juryes impannelled to view
the Delapidacons of the Chancell of the Cathedrall within
Peele Castle, the Chancell of the parish Church of Kk Braddan,
and some other Delapidacòns in and about Bopps Court; We
doe approve of and confirme the same, and doe herby order
the Executor or Executors of the late Lo. Bopp Bridgman
forthwith to make full and Satisfactory payment of the Sumes
of money Sett downe and awarded in the said Returnes, in the
whole amounting to Seaventie five pounds fourteen shillings
and two pence, unto Dr Lake present Lo. Bopp of this Isle
according to our honorble Lords Speciall order in that behalfe.

And whereas Mr. Jon Parr as Atturney for the said Lo.
Bopp hath moved for the paymt of thirtie pounds wch a Jury
of workemen have Sett downe for the takeing downe &
reedifieing of parte of the Tower att Bopps Court, and for

some other moneyes for further Repaires in and about the same place, wee have alsoe taken the same into due consideracon, and finding that by the Custome and usage of this Island the said Executor or Executors are not obliged to the takeing downe and Reedifieing of the said parte of the Tower as the said Jury have declared, only ought to putt the Same in Such ordinary and Sufficient Repair as hitherto hath been accustomed to be done; Therefore wee have thought fitt att present to acquitt and discharge ye sd Executor or Executors or any other that shall or may be concerned for the same from being obliged to take downe and Reedifie the said parte of the Tower according to the verdict of the said Jury; Yett nevertheless doe order and adjudge yt ye said Executor or Executors doe putt the said parte of ye Tower the ffences and other perticulars menconed on Record (and not included in the fore-menconed Sume) in Such necessary & Tenentable repair, as they have hitherto been accustomed to be kept and maintained in, to which the said Executor hath condiscended & given her verball engagemt for the doeing and pforming of the same att any time hereafter when She shall be thereunto desired or required.

Given under our hands att Castletowne
the Seventh day of August Anno Doni 1684.

R. HEYWOOD
THO. NORRIS
FFERD. CALCOTT
THO. NORRIS.

Forasmuch as the Rt Revnd Father in God Baptist Lord Bp of my Isle of Man hath presented unto me a view wch hath heen made of the decays and delapidations of the Chancell of the Cathedrall in my Castle of Peel within my said Isle, Wherein ye Jury and workemen who made the said view have allowed the summ of fourty three pounds nineteen shillings

and ten pence for the making up and repairing of the said
delapidacons, and for that his Ldship (amongst other his good
and zealous designes for the advantage of my said Island) hath
heen fully purposed to bestow and disburse ye said summ of
moneys upon the repaires afore-said but withall considering
that the same would be alltogether ineffectuall, whiles the body
of the Church did lie open and uncovered wch would make
the said Chancell obnoxious to the weather, and endanger the
Same to be blown away with every tempest; And I myself being
upon the place in Summer last, and seeing the said
inconveniency; I have thought it therefore more expedient for
the present. And I do accordingly direct and order, that the said
Summ of fourty three pounds nineteen shillings and ten pence
shall remaine deposited in the hands of ye said Ld Bpp untill it
shall please God to raise some good Instruments and
Benefactors to contribute towards repairing ye whole Church
(the Parishiors who are obliged to do the same being
alltogether unable for the worke) or untill such time as some
good Law shall he made in the sd Island for demolishing of the
said Cathedrall, and the repairing and enlarging of St Peters
Chappell in Peele town with the Materialls thereoff; And if the
same doth not happen or fall out (as it is heartily wished that
it might) in the time of the said Ld Bpp, that then his Lopp
paying the said moneys into the hands of his Successor to the
use & design before mention'd, is to he acquitted and
discharged for ye same or any Obligaon that might lie upon his
Lopp for or concerning the said repaires. And I do direct and
appoint that this my Order shall be entred into the Records of
my said Isle, as well for the satisfaction and discharge of the
said Ld Bp, as the Manifesting of this my present will and
pleasure in, and concerning the premises. Given under my
hand and Seale at Knowsley the 18th day of October in ye yeare
of our Lord God 1686.

                                                    DERBY.

"Whereas by my former Order, hearing date the 18th day of Occobr 1686 I did direct and appoint that the summ of fourty three pounds nineteen shillings and ten pence, wch was allow'd for the repaires of the Chancell of the decay'd Cathedrall Church in Peele Castle within my Isle of Mann shall remain deposited in the hands of ye Rt Revnd Father in God Baptist Ld Bp of my said Isle, untill it should please God to raise some good Instruments and Benefectors to contribute towards ye repairing of the whole Body of the said Cathedrall (the parishionrs who are obliged to do the same heing alltogether unable to contribute to ye sd work) or untill such time as some good law shall he made in my said Island for the demolishing of the said Cathedrall and the repairing and enlarging of St Peters Chappll at Peele Town with the materials thereoff &c. And now forasmuch as the saide summ of fourty three pounds nineteen shillings and ten pence lies still deposited in the Ld Bopps hands, being no way imployed or laid out by him since the receipt thereoff; And allso for that there is nothing expressly mentioned in my said Order, whereby his Lopp is freed and discharg'd from paying any Interest out of the said money whiles it so remains deposited in his hands, wch notwithstanding was intended and intimated by my said Order; yet for the said Ld Bpp further satisfaction in that particular; I do hereby Order and declare that no Interest is to be paid or answered for by the sd Ld Bpp out of the said money, neither for the time past or to come, whiles the same doth continue and remain in the said Bps hands, in regard that he makes no advantage thereoff as afore said. And it is my will and pleasure, and I do further Order and declare, that if ye said Ld Bp, and ye Governour of my saide Isle for the time being, shall at any time hereafter find out some expedient whereby ye said money may be laid out to Interest and well secured, that then it shall be in their power jointly to imploy and lay out the said money to the best advantage and in the securest manner they can to their best judgements and discretion, and wt Interest shall yearly arise or acrew out of the same, that it go towards the advancing of the said Principall summ: And thereupon the said Ld Bp is to be acquitted and discharged from the same for ever afterwards to all intents and purposes whatsoever, any thing contein'd in my said former Order to the contrary thereoff notwithstanding. Given under my hand and Seale at Castle Rushin within my said Isle the 7th day of July Anno Doni 1691.

DERBY.

This is A true Copy
JOSIAH PULLEN
ROBERT HYDE.

—————

APPENDIX I.
(See Note 69, p. 115 supra.)

—————

Letter from Bishop Barrow to the Quakers in the Isle of Man,
from the Exchequer Book, Isle of Man.

LIBER SCAC.⎫
1664—1668, ⎬
p. 59.   ⎭

My Lo. Bishop's Letter to ye Quakers.

My good friends, for soe I desire you would bee, I am not a little troubled to see yu run on in this wilfull way to yor own ruin. Being called upon by God's p.vidence to ye care of this Church I must look upon you as a part of my charge. And though I have hitherto acted only ye part of a governor in outward appearance yett have not ceased to pray dayly for you and doo now exhort you in ye spirit of meekness to consider, as you will answer it at ye day of Judgmt, whether you doo not sine against God in refusing to obey ye lawful comands of Magistrates whom God's p.vidence hath set over you, when the Apostle expressly comands, let every soule bee subject to ye higher powers, telling us the danger of the sine in ye following words,—"hee yt resists shall receive to himself damnac'on."

2ely consider yor sine in withdrawing yor obedience from ye Church when ye Apostle comands also, obey yem which are over you in ye Lord and watch for yor soules. And wthall consider that these 2 sines of rebellion and schism, are reckoned by ye Apostle amongst those yt exclude us from entering into ye kingdom of Heaven. Consider againe yor sine of neglecting yor Estates, and not p.viding for yor families, when ye Apostle tells us that such is worse than Infidells; All you give in Answer for these things is yt you doe according to yor conscience, but, I must tell you, that ye testymoney of conscience must arise from ye conformitie your acc'ons carry wth ye dictates of reason, or ye word of God; Now yor acc'ons are contrary to both, as ye places above menc'oned prove. And therefore yor conscience can be no excuse. Againe consider how you dispise the ministry of ye Church and soe become guilty of despiseing (as ye Apostle) not man but God, for soe saith our Saviour, hee that heareth you heareth mee, and he that despiseth you despiseth mee, and him that sent me. Againe you neglect God's Ordinances, the Sacramts without wch there is no ordinary means of salvac'on. Againe you take upon you to interprett Scripture according to your own ffancies forsaking ye doctrine of the Church wch ye Apostle calls ye ground of truth and wthall tells us that no Scripture is of any privat interpretac'on and St. Peter shews us ye danger of privat interpretac'on, saying yt in ye scripture is many things hard to be understood wch Ignorant and unlearned men wrest to their own destruc'on. Againe you forsake ye publique meeting of Christians, that sine wch ye Apostle reprehends in ye Corinthians, and you must not thinke yt will prove an excuse wch you usually say, that you cannot join wth wicked men in worsp of God; this hath too much of the Pharisee in itt who thanked God yt hee was not as other extorc'onrs &c nor as yt publican wch yett in God's sight was justyfied before him; but you must remember yt the Church by our Saviour is compared unto a nett gathering both good and bad, and we must not forsake ye good because ye badd are amonge them, nor root up ye wheat because of Tares growing up with itt. Itt is not wee that must make ye sep.rac'on itt is ye Angells work this, at yt great harvest day & end of ye world. I beseech you therfore brethren in ye name of God that as you love your own soules (for I speak in love to yem knowing ye price of yem to be ye blood of God) that you make haste to escape out of ye snares of ye devill by wcb he holds you captive & soe long as hee can fasten any one cord upon you hee will not make itt his business to temp you to those open sines of drunkeness, swearing & other debocheries to wch hee see you averse, for hee knows this one sine of spirituall pride (as itt threw him down fro' heaven) soe it will keep you from coming there, beware therefore of his devices for he transforms himself into an Angell of Light yett he is a devill still; Make haste to return to ye Church wch is ready to imbrace you. and earnestly invites you. And believe though I have been forc'd to use rigour wth you to p'serve ye rest of ye flock (wch are my charge also) yett you sall ever find me

> You most loving ffriend & faithfull
> servant in our comon Lord & Saviour

Mat. 18. 7.   ISAAC, SOD. & MAN.

Offences must come saith our Saviour,
tumults & divissions in ye Church,

but woe shall be to yem by whome
they come, hear wt I say & ye Lord
give you understanding.

Copie vera. p. me

RICH FFOX

Ep: Regr

[NOTE.—Dr. Barrow, at the time of writing the above letter
(probably 1663), was Governor as well as Bishop of the Isle
of Man, he having been sent over in the former capacity by
the Earl of Derby, in that year—the year of his
consecration.—EDIT.]

INDEX.